the

H
A
R
D

— *BREAK* —

AARON EDELHEIT

the

H
A
R
D

— BREAK —

The Case for a

24/6 Lifestyle

IDEAPRESS
PUBLISHING

Published in the United States by Ideapress Publishing.

IDEAPRESS PUBLISHING | WWW.IDEAPRESSPUBLISHING.COM

All trademarks are the property of their respective companies.

COVER DESIGN BY FACEOUT STUDIOS

Cataloging-in-Publication Data is on file with the Library of Congress.
ISBN: 978-1-940858-49-4

PROUDLY PRINTED IN THE UNITED STATES OF AMERICA
BY SELBY MARKETING ASSOCIATES

SPECIAL SALES

Ideapress Books are available at a special discount for bulk purchases for sales promotions and premiums, or for use in corporate training programs. Special editions, including personalized covers, a custom foreword, corporate imprints and bonus content are also available.

I dedicate this book to my partner and best friend in life, Valerie.
Without you this book, would not have been possible.

TABLE OF CONTENTS

PART THREE:
A SUCCESSFUL SABBATH

INTRODUCTION:
ALL THIS AND MORE!

WHAT IF YOU COULD BECOME MORE PRODUCTIVE, CREATIVE, AND INNO-vative? What if you could solve problems faster and easier than ever before, while minimizing mistakes? What if you could be more resilient to the ups and downs of business and life?

What if you could reduce your stress levels, become healthier, and lower your risk of disease and illness? What if you could become happier, improve your family life, and have more time to spend with friends and loved ones? On top of that, what if you could even make your food taste better? And, what if changing just one thing in your life could give you all that and more?

Interested? Intrigued? What's the magic potion? Simple: it's the Sabbath—a tradition that is thousands of years old but has become especially relevant at this moment in history.

Sounds too good to be true, right? But it isn't. Decades of research at dozens of universities—including Harvard and Stanford—plus studies by private companies, and data compiled by government agencies around the world show that taking one day a week to disconnect from work and reconnect with everything else you value will change your life in all the ways described above.

I am a workaholic, and I am just as addicted to my smartphone as everyone else. However, one day every week, I separate myself from work, technology, and schedules. No smartphone, no computer, and no rush. I don't send or answer emails or texts. I try not to talk about business. And I don't race around trying to complete other non-work activities. In other words, one day a week, I just choose not to be busy.

It wasn't easy for me. While not physically hard, a Sabbath from work and over-scheduled activities is mentally challenging. In fact, as an ambitious and driven person, I initially thought the idea of not working so unfathomable that it seemed almost alien. But now, it has become the foundational habit of my life. This book is a tribute—a love letter, if you will—to the regular practice of taking a hard break from the frenetic craziness of modern life and retreating into an oasis that sustains me.

My goal in writing this book is to change the way people view and experience their modern lives. I will offer a different perspective and concrete guidelines that can make people more productive at work, bring them greater happiness, save their marriages, and improve the overall quality of their lives.

I want to bring about a change in our culture, and I will show how this is possible by telling stories of the dramatic change I have undergone in my own life, and about similar changes experienced by some very successful business leaders. And I will present an abundance of compelling scientific research that clearly demonstrates the transformative value of the Sabbath concept.

This book is divided into three parts. In Part One, "The 24/7 Life," I share research and studies that show how detrimental overwork is to productivity, safety, and health. In Part Two, "The Value of a Hard Break," I tell stories and present research that show how much healthier, happier, more creative, and more productive people and organizational cultures are when they build regular rest and relaxation into their lives. Finally, in Part Three, "A Successful Sabbath," I will walk you step by step through how to prepare for and make the most of a weekly hard break in your life.

I felt compelled to write this book because taking a hard break has changed my life in profound ways. I am Jewish, but many traditions incorporate a Sabbath, and I believe that the benefits of a Sabbath can be shared by everyone, regardless of what religion they belong to, or whether they are religious at all. This book is my best attempt at spreading the value of observing a Sabbath. I hope its message resonates with you, and that a hard break or Sabbath will change your life like it has mine.

Enjoy,
Aaron Edelheit

PART ONE

THE
24/7
LIFE

CHAPTER 1

TEARS

Beware the barrenness of a busy life.

— SOCRATES

TEARS ROLLED DOWN MY CHEEKS AS I STOOD IN THE SHOWER. I don't remember how long I was there, only that I sobbed like a child, as uncontrollable waves shook my body. The mental anguish was just too much to handle, and I didn't hold anything back. Everything that seemed important in my life had gone wrong, and I couldn't shake the sense of disappointment in myself. It was July 2003. How had I gotten to this point? What had gone wrong?

Just six months earlier, I had been on top of the world. In four short years as a money manager, I'd racked up a stellar track record, averaging annual returns of greater than 25 percent. What was remarkable was that it happened between 1998 and 2002, when the market struggled and most investors struggled along with it. My investors were happy and starting to invest more, and I was beginning to attract real attention. I had taken on a business partner, and was imagining a future as a big-time hedge- fund manager.

Not bad for a 28-year-old who had started in a bedroom above his parents' garage. I had been dreaming of managing money and investing in the stock market ever since I was 14, growing up in South Florida and idolizing Peter Lynch, the famed manager of Fidelity's Magellan Fund. To top it off, I had recently fallen in love, and all seemed right with the world.

But even with all my good fortune, something felt off. I couldn't put my finger on it. Despite working seven days a week, building a business, and making my investors and myself rich, something was missing. What was it?

I thought it might be spiritual. I had been raised Jewish, but aside from the annual ritual of High Holiday services (Rosh Hashanah and Yom Kippur) and a Passover Seder, I was not particularly observant. In December of 2002, I decided to check out Friday night services at a local synagogue in Atlanta, where I had been living after attending high school and college in Georgia. The rabbi who led the services was insightful and funny, and I connected with him emotionally.

While he was almost everything one could want in a religious leader, at the end of the day, I realized I didn't want to go services every Friday night. I wasn't sure that I really wanted to be religious. I did join the young professionals group at the synagogue, believing that what I was missing might be a community. But I felt lost there, and never really engaged with the group.

Then I fell in love with a wonderful woman, a friend from college. When we fell in love, it was such a joyous, intense experience, I thought it was love that had been missing from my life. We lived in different cities, but we traveled to see each other, and tried to figure out how to make the long-distance relationship work.

When the new year of 2003 began, everything looked like sunshine and rainbows, but by March, my investment portfolio had started to underperform. I couldn't figure out what was wrong. I wasn't experienced or wise enough to realize that everyone underperforms at some point. This was simply the life of investors, especially successful ones. Even Warren Buffett had extended periods of underperformance.

I doubled down on work with more research, deeper dives into due diligence, and more conversations with executives at potential investments. I was toiling away, always trying to get more information. Where I had previously been working 70 hours a week, now it was 90 or 100. Surely, more time and effort would help. But it didn't.

Then I started fighting with my new business partner. Underperformance and a dysfunctional business relationship made my work life hurt like it never had before. That was when my brief adventure in love came to an end. The physical distance between us, combined with my own immaturity, caused the relationship to collapse. I also think the pressure I felt from my business didn't help at all, or the fact that I had zero perspective on the relative importance of my work.

To cap off my misfortune, in late March, I suddenly started experiencing severe pain throughout my abdomen. I had always been a high-energy (read: high-stress) person. I had been taking Nexium to treat acid reflux for over a year, but this pain was different. When I ended up in the emergency room, the first doctor told me I needed to reduce my stress, and that I might have pulled a stomach muscle. The next doctor ordered examinations of my upper and lower gastrointestinal tract. They showed nothing.

When yet another visit to the emergency room provided no relief, I began to think I was imagining the symptoms. The fourth doctor said, "I don't know what is wrong with you, but let's rule out as much as we can." It wasn't my heart. It wasn't my colon. It wasn't my prostate (the number of times I was asked to bend over to have my prostate checked still gives me the sweats.) The pain was appearing all over my stomach and abdomen, so apparently, the doctors were trying to cover all the bases. Again … nothing.

After two weeks, I was hunched over in pain, barely able to eat anything but crackers and water, and didn't know what to do. One night, I woke up in startling pain and knew that something was very wrong. My best friend drove me to the hospital at 2:00 a.m. as I struggled to breathe.

In the emergency room, they clearly saw that I was in a medical crisis and gave me pain medication while they did blood tests and a CT scan. Suddenly, a doctor showed up and told me my appendix was exploding and that it had to be removed immediately. To this day, I remember my jubilation at knowing that I wasn't insane, and that I had something that could be fixed. I remember joking with the nurses who, deathly quiet, wheeled me to pre-surgery and telling them about all the fried chicken and lasagna I planned to eat after the surgery.

As it turned out, the surgeon had to remove not only my appendix, but also a portion of my colon that had been affected by the poison leaking from my appendix. I was told that my appendicitis was atypical, and it wasn't until it was quite advanced that the pain became localized to the bottom-right side of my abdomen. That explained why no one had been able to diagnose the problem.

Although I had been clearly advised by my doctors to take it easy, as my recovery would take a few months, I tried to get back into the swing of things in a matter of days. That didn't go well. The disagreements with my business partner escalated into arguments over expenses and credit-card bills. In May, we parted ways, after having been friends for seven years.

So, there I was, alone again, both professionally and personally. I felt empty, and was losing money for my investors while the market was soaring. There was no one and nothing to fall back on. I felt alone and trapped. That was when I found myself crying in the shower.

Would you like to know the extent of the losses that drove me to such desperation? Five percent. A measly five percentage points had my life careening off the rails. I didn't know how to deal with my own disappointment and failure. Famed investor Seth Klarman wrote in his book *Margin of Safety,* "Investment returns are not a direct function of how long or hard you work or how much you wish to earn." I wish I had read that quote back then. Nevertheless, my depression turned out to be one of the best things that had ever happened to me, because it made me realize that more hours worked did not equal more success.

Much later, I found out that it is common for people to experience depression and mood swings after major surgery. But I knew that this was more than that. I realized that something in my life was fundamentally out of whack. I went and found a therapist to talk to. That started a period of introspection about my life, and led me to the realization that I needed to change. Working 24/7 didn't appear to be helping my business or personal life. What could I do?

CHAPTER 2

WORK LESS, PRODUCE MORE

Quality is more important than quantity.

—STEVE JOBS

The concept of overwork is an old one, dating back to 1530, when "overworke" meant "to cause to work too hard." As John Palsgrave, a tutor in the royal house of King Henry VIII, wrote that year, "Whan I overworke myselfe I am the werier two dayes after."[1]

That people have been working themselves to their limits for hundreds of years is no real surprise. Working hard and striving for more is in our nature, and unless you win the lottery, it's hard to accomplish anything without hard work. Think of the famous quote by Thomas Edison, "Genius is one percent inspiration and 99 percent perspiration."

And look at how today's business titans are fawned over and lionized for their work habits. Driven, motivated people, such as Elon Musk and Jeff

Bezos, and past business titans like Edison and John Rockefeller, have helped reinforce the idea that to get ahead, you need to put in Herculean hours and constantly push yourself. That success is simply the result of hard work is treated as common knowledge.

Much ink has been spilled on work, work habits, productivity, work hours, and overwork. There are countless books on how to work more and effectively, get more organized, network better, climb the corporate ladder, start your own business, become a leader, and the like. Just reading these books can be work! Even though many are insightful, a lot of their advice about how to succeed boils down to working hard and showing others how hard you work. This belief has led to a big change in how people talk about themselves.

"I'm overwhelmed at work."
"I worked on Saturday and Sunday last weekend."
"I have hundreds of emails in my inbox."
"I'm so busy."

The Productivity Myth

Working hard and talking about how hard one works have become societal cues. "Look at me! Look how busy I am!" Just as a peacock spreads its feathers, people now throw out comments and indicators of their busyness, importance, and the importance of their work.

Peer pressure at the office can be a powerful social motivator. Comments or slight digs at fellow workers who leave early or don't seem to be putting in the same hours are common. In fact, many employees try to signal to their bosses how hard they work by virtually camping out at the office. Being seen putting in long hours can, for many employees, seem more important than working effectively.

I have seen many examples of this in my career. Several people I know revel in long hours and the consumption of massive amounts of caffeine. As I described in the previous chapter, I used to be as guilty as anyone of celebrating long hours. I remember taking a picture of a parking lot that was empty except for my car, and thinking proudly of how hard a worker I was. I also remember not sleeping one night, and thinking I was being a hero.

What are the results of all this hard work? Are people more productive? Do they deliver better results?

Philosophers and economists have long theorized that if people worked fewer hours, they would be more productive. Adam Smith said, "The man who works so moderately as to be able to work constantly, not only preserves his health the longest, but in the course of the year, executes the greatest quantity of works." The 20th-century philosopher Bertrand Russell argued that people should only work four hours a day, to experience "happiness and joy of life, instead of frayed nerves, weariness and dyspepsia."

How do you prove such an argument? And what is the right number of hours to work? Is it really four hours a day, as Russell argued? John Pencavel, a professor at Stanford University, has studied this very question. His landmark research was based on a treasure trove of data from the study of British munitions workers during World War I.[2]

When World War I started, Britain suspended all the existing labor laws that had been put in place to protect workers. The country was at war, and needed the highest level of production possible. The British formed a government commission to determine how to increase the production of weapons and munitions. That commission's recommendations are as shocking today as they probably were back then.

The commission concluded that workers needed to work less, not more. Professor Pencavel was fascinated by the commission's conclusions, and scrutinized their data and calculations to see if their analysis was reliable. He found that the data was extensive, and their calculations were spot on. Pencavel confirmed that when munitions workers put in more than 50 hours a week, output rose at a decreasing rate. Even more dramatic was the evidence that the output was the same whether a person worked 56 or 70 hours.

Once you get past the shock, it makes sense, doesn't it? The more we work, the more tired we become, and the harder it is to focus our attention. Other studies have corroborated this fact. Some of them even go back to cotton mills in the nineteenth century. In fact, the trend toward limiting the workweek to 40 hours came not only from the labor movement, but also from employers like Henry Ford. Ford and other business leaders realized that increasing work hours beyond a certain point led to decreasing productivity and quality. Why pay for more hours, if those hours produced diminishing returns?[3]

Some Countries Are More Productive Than Others

Let's look at hours worked and productivity a different way—from the perspective of countries as a whole. There is excellent country-level data about working habits. It turns out that the Greeks are some of the hardest-working people in the EU in terms of hours on the job. On average, they put in more than 2,000 hours a year. Germans, however, clock only about 1,400 hours a year. But which workforce is more productive? No offense to the Greeks, but German workers' productivity is about 70 percent higher—even with substantially fewer hours.

The average American works over 400 more hours per year than the average German. Yet the two countries have remarkably similar economic outputs (based on gross domestic product). More hours worked clearly does not mean more economic output.[4] It wasn't always like this. In the 1970s, Americans and Europeans worked approximately the same number of hours,[5] but, now we work more hours per capita for basically the same result.

Perhaps the most interesting conclusion from Pencavel's research into British munitions workers in World War I was the fact that those who worked a six-day schedule, with a break for the Sabbath (Sunday, in Britain), achieved a total output 10 percent higher than those who worked a seven-day schedule. So here is evidence that increased productivity is not just a matter of fewer hours, but of having a hard break each week, as well. Again, this makes intuitive sense. If you have a regular day off, you will be more refreshed than someone who works every day.

CHAPTER 3

ERRORS BOTH
LARGE AND SMALL

*To make no mistakes is not in the power of man; but from their errors
and mistakes the wise and good learn wisdom for the future.*

—PLUTARCH

The Grave Consequences of Fatigue

Four minutes and 55 seconds remained before the launch of the Space Shuttle Columbia on January 6, 1986. Unknown to mission command, 18,000 pounds of liquid oxygen had inadvertently been drained from the Shuttle external tank due to operator error.[6] Fortunately for the seven-person crew, a mere 31 seconds before liftoff, an alarm went off letting everyone know that the temperature in the main engine had dropped below the acceptable limit. If launched, the shuttle would not have reached orbit, with tragic results.

An investigation found that fatigue led mission control operators to misinterpret a system error message, which caused them to mistakenly vent the liquid oxygen. When they did so, they had already been on duty for 11 hours on their third 12-hour, 8:00 p.m. to 8:00 a.m., shift in a row.

Six days later, Columbia took off successfully, and all was well.

The workload demands surrounding a shuttle launch for the ground crew and Mission Control at Kennedy Space Center can be grueling, and can induce pressure to work beyond reasonable overtime limits, especially during delays and within the last few days before liftoff. A later investigation found that there had been 149 instances of employees working 40 hours or more of overtime, including two employees who worked almost 100 hours in one week.

On January 27, 1986, about two weeks after the Columbia's launch, a critical conference call took place between NASA and their aerospace contractors. The decision at hand was whether to go ahead with the scheduled launch of the Space Shuttle Challenger the next day, or delay the mission due to cold weather. What would be the effect of abnormally low temperatures on the solid rocket booster joint? During that critical conference call, exhausted NASA employees and contractors argued over whether to go forward with the mission, and there was "a clear opportunity for postponement." Later, the Presidential Commission Report said the following:

> Time pressure, particularly caused by launch scrubs and rapid turnarounds, increases the potential for sleep loss and judgment errors. This could be minimized by preventing launch support personnel, particularly managers, from combining launch support duty with office work on the same day. The willingness of NASA employees in general to work excessive hours, while

admirable, raises serious questions when it jeopardizes job performance, particularly when critical management decisions are at stake.

Nonetheless, the decision was made to launch the Space Shuttle Challenger on schedule. During the launch on January 28, 1986, an O-ring on the solid rocket booster failed to seal, and the Space Shuttle Challenger exploded—tragically killing all seven astronauts on board and setting the space program back decades.

Beyond the lack of productivity caused by overwork, there is another negative outcome: errors. Some are large and catastrophic, such as the Challenger explosion, and some are small, like sending an email to the wrong person. Organizations and companies that rely on overworking their employees may not realize how many errors they are encouraging.

Long hours typify certain jobs, and research has documented the unintended consequences of those long hours. In a study of hospital staff nurses, shifts longer than 12 hours and workweeks longer than 40 hours were associated with significantly heightened probabilities of error, and have raised questions about patient safety.[7]

It should surprise no one that a study found that medical interns were significantly more likely to be involved in motor vehicle crashes if they had just worked extended shifts. Similar reports have been made about airline pilots, police officers, truck drivers, and soldiers.

Even more important than traffic accidents are what medical interns or nurses may do during their long working hours. The third leading cause of death in this country is medical errors. Over 250,000 people are estimated to die every year because of medical errors, according to a study by Johns Hopkins Medicine.[8]

Outside the medical field, an analysis of more than 10,000 workers between 1987 and 2000 found that, holding several other factors constant, those who worked at least 12 hours each day had injury hazard rates that were 37 percent higher than those who did not, and those who worked at least 60 hours per week were 23 percent higher.[9]

Truck drivers who drive more than eight hours a day are twice as likely to experience a crash as those who drive less.[10] More than 4,000 people in the U.S. die every year in crashes involving trucks. This data drove the Department of Transportation to issue new hours-of-service rules in 2011. These rules reduced the total number of hours truckers may drive in a week from 82 to 70. The rules also require drivers to take a 30-minute break during the first eight hours of a shift, and to rest for a minimum of 34 hours after a 70-hour workweek.[11]

Fatigue Affects Soft Skills, Too

Sleep and breaks are important for injury and mistake prevention, but a lack of breaks also leads to poorer interpersonal skills. According to studies cited in the *Harvard Business Review,* when we overwork, we tend to misread people's faces negatively: happy faces are more likely to look neutral, and neutral faces are more likely to look like frowning faces. We are also quicker to lash out at perceived insults. Since reading facial expressions and controlling emotions are so crucial to leadership roles, when we overwork, we are impairing our ability to lead.[12]

A Centers for Disease Control (CDC) overview of approximately 50 different studies found that extended work periods (more than 40 hours a week) decreased physical and cognitive performance.[13] Other studies from the United Auto Workers and Procter & Gamble found that overtime led to poorer cognitive performance from employees. A 2008 study from Finland showed that work without rest caused workers to demonstrate "lower cognitive function, including poor vocabulary and reasoning."[14] And it's not just short-term performance that is affected. Overworking has been shown to lead to a drop in long-term cognitive performance after just five years of overwork.[15]

Despite the overwhelming data, company cultures still focus on the look and feel of work, not the actual quality. As a society, instead of receiving benefits, we are getting errors, poor performance, and injuries.

CHAPTER 4

WHY DON'T AMERICANS LIKE GOING ON VACATION?

No man needs a vacation so much as the man who has just had one.
—ELBERT HUBBARD

The purpose of a vacation is to take a break from work, renewing mind and body. People use this time for fun, rest, spending time with family, traveling, and having new experiences. Personally, I love the sense of adventure that comes from being on vacation in some new location. I also love the sense of freedom of resetting my daily routine and not being on the clock.

Besides having to offer vacation for legal reasons such as national holidays, business owners recognize that employees need a break to refresh and avoid burn-out. It's essential for the long-term success of any business.

662 Million Unused Vacation Days

Since the travel industry makes its money from vacations, they routinely conduct detailed studies of how American workers use their vacation time. The industry's initiative, named Project: Time Off, estimates that in one recent year, Americans left 662 million paid vacation days unused, and forfeited 206 million vacation days that could not be rolled over or paid out. Workers used an average of 16.8 vacation days in 2016, well below the average of 20.3 logged from 1976 to 2000.[16]

Even when people do take vacations, thanks to the technology that now connects us 24/7, they aren't really leaving work. Some people take "workcations," and work from a remote location while supposedly on vacation. Are they really on vacation, or just at work with a change of scenery? I remember working even on my honeymoon in Hawaii, in 2010. I'm not talking about a little work, but a lot. I had a portfolio to manage, and I was trying to claw back losses from the financial crisis of 2008 and 2009 while also attempting to grow my side project, a single-family rental home business. I felt pressure not to let those things slide, even on my honeymoon. Consequently, my honeymoon did not feel like a vacation. There we were in Hawaii, and for five or six hours a day, I would pound away at work. My wife had a bad cold after our wedding, and recovered on our honeymoon by sleeping 14 hours a day. I remember feeling relief that while she was resting and recovering, I could take care of business. Thankfully for me, though, and for my new wife, there was one Sabbath during our honeymoon, and guess what? I couldn't work on that day. I did work every other day, though. I struggle even today with the same issues of feeling driven to work as I did then. But that honeymoon Sabbath was a line in the sand that even my worst tendencies couldn't cross.

Why was I working so much?

Smartphone users spend an average of five hours on work emails every weekend, reports the Center for Creative Leadership. Some of us spend much more than that. A poll by the employment website Glassdoor found that 66 percent of people have worked during a vacation.[17]

Fear drives people to work while on vacation. The financial crisis still reverberates in our collective consciousness. People don't want to get behind in their work. They want to show how important they are, and don't want to be viewed in a negative light by their bosses.[18] Employees fear they will be penalized for taking time off. One study showed that a whopping 57 percent of employees surveyed reported some degree of difficulty in taking time off because of their work culture.[19]

Lonnie Golden, a professor at Penn State University who studies vacation and the workplace, says, "There is workplace peer pressure to minimize using time off." He explains that a company may offer a generous vacation package, but everyone who works at the company knows that you need to get the work done. "If you leave your work for a week or two, you feel like [work] will just pile up."[20]

One of the best executives I've ever worked with was a working mother of four children, who, because of her need and desire to be home with her family, rarely worked more than 45 hours a week. I was more than happy to accommodate her family's schedule, because I knew the quality of her work was so high. But in a culture of too many companies, going home at a reasonable hour is seen as leaving work "early," and is frowned upon. The pressure to be seen at the office is an attitude that really should be eradicated from corporate life.

"No One Knows Where I Am"

A truly comical aspect of the culture of overwork is that most companies cannot even tell who is overworking and who is simply pretending! Consider a 2010 study from the University of California that surveyed 39 corporate managers who reported that those employees who spent more time in the office were "more dedicated, more hardworking and more responsible."[21] And yet a Boston University study of 115 managers found that these managers could not correctly identify which employees worked 80 hours and which ones only pretended to work 80 hours. A few employees used ingenious tactics—such as telecommuting and keeping their exact location secret—to keep fellow workers and managers in the dark. "I skied five days last week … no one knows where I am," one said. His colleagues viewed him as a rising star.[22]

Employees who asked openly for reduced work hours or accommodations, so they could help with child care were penalized or marginalized in some way. Appearances are what matter, not actual work quality. Remember what managers said about employees who work long hours. They did not mention whether they were more productive or more effective.

Another powerful reason people don't take time off is that it is so easy to work remotely. Thanks to technology, it has never been easier be in contact with co-workers, clients, investors, etc. When you post on Instagram, Facebook, or Twitter while on vacation, "you are only one button away from work," says Rusty Rueff, a career and workplace expert at the employment review site Glassdoor.[23]

Guilt is another factor. Business owner David Demming of Demming Financial Services felt so guilty about taking vacations that he didn't take one for 15 years, and only started then because he could take clients along to combine work and vacation.[24]

What do you notice about the reasons people aren't taking more vacations? They have nothing to do with the quality of their work, creativity, or innovation. They are not based in fact, but in negative emotions like fear and guilt. Professor Pencavel's work at Stanford has already shown us that working more than 50 hours a week doesn't accomplish anything positive. We also know from Germany that the productivity of a workforce has no direct relation to the number of hours worked. By the way, Germany has one of the world's best-mandated vacation policies with 29 paid vacation days a year, which Germans are only too happy to use—unlike Americans.

CHAPTER 5

WHY ARE WE OVERWORKING AND OVERSCHEDULING OURSELVES?

If unwilling to rise in the morning, say to thyself,
"I awake to do the work of a man."

—MARCUS AURELIUS

Unused vacation time and workcations are just one piece of the puzzle. Why in the world are people acting this way when the evidence is so firmly against it? We will examine the reasons in this chapter: the working rich; overwork as status symbol; overwork as a form of heroism; the leaky nature of work; fear of becoming non-essential; and a very real psychological phenomenon called the Zeigarnik effect.

The Working Rich

The rich are now likely to work more hours than the poor. In 2002, the top 20 percent of earners were twice as likely to work more than 50 hours a week than the bottom 20 percent.[25] This is a reversal of historic proportions. Isn't the whole point of being rich that you can work less and have more time for leisure and travel? Time travelers from even the recent past would be baffled at the current behavior of the one percent.

Why does *The Wall Street Journal* have to write an article filled with tips for leaving work behind when on vacation? The average **WSJ** reader has a household income of $272,000 and a net worth of $1.4 million.[26] Shouldn't these people be enjoying the high life, having lots of free time and taking vacations galore?

Another recent **WSJ** article is very telling. "Why 4 a.m. Is the Most Productive Hour," lauds executive after executive for their early wake-up habits.[27]

Four a.m. to 6:00 a.m. is "the most planned, most organized and most scheduled part of my day. It's a crapshoot from there," says one executive quoted in the article. "I feel like I get a head start on everybody," he says. Another executive quoted in the article says he can think more clearly when he goes for a 4:00 a.m. run, because he doesn't have to dodge other people. One of my favorite statements in the article is, "The coffee starts making itself at 3:45 a.m." Just to be clear, the coffee doesn't make itself; the coffee machine makes the coffee, because the human owner of the coffee machine programmed it to do so. Might I suggest the human may also be a bit more programmed than necessary?

With such focus on extreme schedules, what gets crowded out is unscheduled time, hanging out with friends, spending time creating games with your children, relaxing, and simply reflecting on life.

If getting up at 4:00 a.m. is what they need to do to make it work and they're not compromising their health and family life, more power to them. But the article itself doesn't mention what they do for their downtime or hard break, so it is in danger of spreading the gospel of overwork by representing these high-achieving early-risers as role models.

Overwork as Status Symbol

The *wsj* article is an example of social cues and pressure signaling. The newspaper that most exemplifies success and wealth publishes an article suggesting readers wake up at 4:00 a.m., and the implication is that if they do so, they will be successful like the people quoted in the article.

Fifty years ago, leisure signaled wealth. Banks were only open from 10:00 a.m. to 3:00 p.m. until the end of the 1960s. People regularly describe these hours as banker's hours. Bankers were part of the wealthy class, and many rich people followed their example. Now it's busyness that signals wealth. The wealthy display their schedules, wake-up times, and other badges of just how very busy they are. And that encourages people who aspire to be wealthy and successful to be just as busy, if not more so. Researchers at Columbia, Georgetown, and Harvard have found that being busy has become a status symbol that can project one's own importance in our "always-on" world.

A recent *Washington Post* article by Jena McGregor, "How 'Busyness' Became a Bona Fide Status Symbol," has this to say regarding the current research:

In experiments, they found that participants thought of people who were described as working longer hours as having higher status. They also tended to put brands or products that offer convenience or multi-tasking on a level with those known simply for being expensive.

"Luxury goods are losing signaling value" as more people can afford them, said Silvia Bellezza, a professor of marketing at Columbia University who co-authored the paper. Talking about a scarcity of time is "a more nuanced way to display [importance] that doesn't go through conspicuous consumption. It's implicitly telling you that 'I am very important, and my human capital is sought after, which is why I'm so busy.'"

... Again, and again, participants rated the person who worked more as having more social status, even when the person researchers asked about was thought to work slowly. In other words, getting the work done fast and having more time for leisure was not something associated with prestige.[28]

Call me a contrarian, but I get a little queasy when something gets too fashionable. Something is very wrong with this picture. Stepping back, we can see that extreme schedules and work habits, while they may be ways to signal high status, don't actually lead to high work quality, innovation, creativity, efficiency, or making good decisions. In fact, as we've discussed, they tend to lead to the opposite.

Heroes Don't Sleep

Another important publication that tackles this issue is the *Harvard Business Review*. In 2013, they published an article entitled, "Why Men Work So Many Hours" by Joan C. Williams, distinguished professor of law and founding director of the Center of WorkLife Law at the University of California, Hastings College of the Law. In the article, Williams cites research comparing the working hours of men and women, and even more specifically, working mothers and fathers. The article states:

> Working long hours is a "heroic activity," noted Cynthia Fuchs Epstein and her co-authors in their 1999 study of lawyers. Marianne Cooper's study of engineers in Silicon Valley closely observes how working long hours turns pencil pushing or computer keyboarding into a manly test of physical endurance. "There's a kind of machismo culture that you don't sleep," one participant told her. "Successful enactment of this masculinity," Cooper concludes, "involves displaying one's exhaustion, physically and verbally, to convey the depth of one's commitment, stamina, and virility."[29]

Men particularly have this problem. Williams writes, "Not only is work devotion a 'class act'—a way of enacting class status—it's also a certain way of being a 'real' man."

Men overwork more than women do. Only nine percent of working women with children and 14 percent of those without children work more than 50 hours a week, according to a 2011 survey by the U.S. Census Bureau. Compare that to 29 percent for men with children and 21 percent for men with no children. These numbers suggest that women realize working long hours doesn't make sense. And yet all one has to do is look at the enduring wage gap between men and women to understand that women are suffering economically for what is ultimately a wiser, healthier relationship to work. They suffer in part because overwork is perceived to have so much value in the culture of so many organizations, and in the culture at large.

Your Work Is Leaking on the Rest of Your Life

Another culprit in the epidemic of overwork in our culture is what *Atlantic* writer Derek Thompson calls the "leaky" nature of modern work.[30] In describing his own work life, Thompson says he spends time working and "facebooking," and doesn't have set hours. He says that he checks Twitter both for work and fun, and that reading a novel can lead to an idea for an article.

Ever pick up your phone on the weekend to check the weather or read a text from a friend and notice you have an email? It's from a work colleague. Next thing you know, 10 to 15 minutes have gone by, and you have forgotten to do the thing you initially picked up the phone to do. You were going to check the weather to see if it was fine to go to the park with your daughter, and next thing you knew, you were working.

Work is always one click away when you are texting with friends, on the phone with a loved one, or sitting on your couch at home with your family. Because so much of our work revolves around communication and our cell phones, it's always there waiting for us; and once you open the door to it, it never ends. We are vigilant against water leaks in our homes because they can lead to all kinds of long-term problems, from mold to structural damage. Work leaking into non-work time can cause equivalent structural damage to our personal lives, so we must be just as vigilant against allowing it to happen.

Fear of Being Non-Essential

There's a story about a big-time partner in a successful law firm who reportedly never took a day off and never went on vacation. A young lawyer asked him, "How come you don't take even one day off?" The partner said, "Well, one of two things could happen when I'm gone, and both are terrible. The first is that the firm could collapse or go into crisis, and without me at the helm, everything I've tried to build could be ruined. The second is that nothing would happen."

There is tremendous insight in this story. Fear of being non-essential drives many people to overwork. It is incredibly humbling to realize the world keeps on spinning without us. Why are we working so hard if everything doesn't collapse when we stop?

We've discussed the fear that drives people to take less vacation time. But there is another kind of fear, a personal fear that what we are doing is inessential, or that we really don't matter.

We all want to make a difference in our lives, and we all want to accomplish things that matter, but what if our work really doesn't make an impact? What if what we are doing is meaningless in the end? This is a scary and humbling thought no matter who we are–a CEO or an unpaid intern.

Just because these thoughts arise doesn't mean we should be working all the time. These kinds of thoughts, while depressing, confront us about the true meaning in our lives. For many years, I struggled with managing money for rich people. What was the purpose of making rich people richer? I eventually came to the conclusion that the money I made enabled me to donate to charitable organizations that were important to me, and that being my own boss allowed me to set hours that enabled me to volunteer my time for worthy causes. But was that good enough? These questions were partly what led me to shut down my hedge fund in 2011 and focus on my real-estate venture, The American Home. I wanted to build something and feel something more tangible than stocks and investments, which felt ephemeral to me.

Beyond work implications, these questions drove me to learn more about my own traditions, and work hard to become a better member of my community. In addition, they further cemented the importance of keeping a Sabbath. These questions about my life's meaning arose out of that initial, fearful question that a lot of us have— *What if my contribution at work is not essential to the survival of the business?* —This propelled me forward, in ways I didn't expect, into deeper questions about how I wanted to spend my brief time on earth.

The Zeigarnik Effect

A final answer to the question of why we overwork may be a psychological phenomenon known as the Zeigarnik effect. Simply stated, the Zeigarnik effect is the tendency to dwell upon and refuse to let go of any task that has not been finished. We must complete a task, or thoughts of its incompletion will intrude as we attempt to focus on something else. This behavior, which appears to be hardwired in our brains, is now made more powerful by our use of smartphones.

In 1927, a Soviet psychologist named Bluma Zeigarnik was sitting in a restaurant in Vienna when she noticed that the waiters there remembered orders that had not yet been completed, but they rapidly forgot the ones they had already brought to the diners' tables. She then conducted a study in which she gave people simple tasks, like solving puzzles or stringing beads. She interrupted them in these tasks some of the time, and when she asked them afterward to remember the tasks, she discovered they were twice as likely to remember the uncompleted tasks as the completed ones.

Since then, scientists have provided further proof of the Zeigarnik effect. Participants in a 1982 study were asked to complete a tough puzzle, but they were interrupted before they could finish, and were told the study was over. Ninety percent of the participants continued to work on the puzzle anyway. They just couldn't let it remain incomplete.[31]

Jennifer Deal, a senior research scientist at the Center for Creative Leadership, says to think of the Zeigarnik effect as that "snippet of a song you can't get out of your head."[32] Because the work of executives, managers, and professionals is rarely finished, people in these types of roles are ripe for being influenced by the Zeigarnik effect. And those with a high need for achievement appear to be even more susceptible to it. While the inability to let unfinished tasks be forgotten has always been with us, "the invasiveness of it has been exacerbated by technology. The increased accessibility to work highlights the possibility of finishing whatever is left undone."

Deal recommends a few strategies to combat the Zeigarnik effect. They include deeply focusing and trying not to multitask. The one that makes the most sense to me is simply "to turn the phone off and put it physically away, even locking it in a safe if you have to. If you can't look at it—that is, you can't without going to substantial trouble—the brain itch will eventually die off because you can't scratch it." Unfortunately, studies and

surveys show that executives and employees keep on scratching that itch …
to their own detriment.

CHAPTER 6

THE TOLL ON OUR HEALTH AND FAMILY

To keep the body in good health is a duty...
otherwise we shall not be able to keep our mind strong and clear.

—BUDDHA

The costs of overwork and stress are reverberating through our economy. A 2016 joint study by Harvard and Stanford estimated the health care costs stemming from work-related stress at somewhere between $125 billion and $190 billion annually. Companies now estimate that 50 percent of employee exits are driven by burnout.[33]

An Easy Way to Induce a Heart Attack

Is anyone interested in an 80 percent increase in coronary risk? Apparently, all you have to do is work 10 or more hours a day, according to a 2012 review of 50 years of research published in the *American Journal of Epidemiology*.[34]

Other studies show that you are 60 percent more likely to have heart-related problems if you work more than 10 hours a day, and 40 percent more likely to have coronary disease than those who work normal hours.[35] Research has also linked overwork to strokes.[36] Women are particularly at risk for long-term health problems. Women who work an average of 60 hours a week are three times as likely as those who work 40 hours to eventually develop heart disease, cancer, arthritis, or diabetes, and more than twice as likely to have chronic lung disease or asthma.[37] Yikes!

And this is not limited to the United States. Marianna Virtanen of the Finnish Institute of Occupational Health has demonstrated a correlation between long work hours, depressive symptoms, and heart disease. She also found a link between long work hours and type 2 diabetes. The risk is especially high for those in low-income categories. Those who overwork are also more likely to become heavy drinkers.[38]

According to a Centers for Disease Control review of more than 50 global studies, the more overtime you put in and the more weeks you work over 40 hours, the more likely it is that you will be in poorer health, at increased risk of injury, and have an increased risk of mortality. Two studies stand out. A German study reviewed 1.2 million injury reports and found that after the eighth or ninth hour of consecutive work, people had a higher risk of injury on the job. Another study found that a combination of 12 hours worked in any one day and over 40 hours a week led to an elevated risk for neck, shoulder, and back disorders.[39]

Then there is the mental health toll. Disability awards for mental disorders have dramatically increased since 1980. Substance abuse, especially of opiates, is at epidemic levels.[40] Mental health problems are becoming a significant burden for society. According to the Partnership for Workplace Mental Health, mental illness and substance abuse cost employers an estimated $80 to $100 billion annually. The World Health Organization has named depression as the number-one disease burden for the economy worldwide.[41]

The problem seems to be getting worse for millennials. According to a recent report by the American Psychological Association and Harris Interactive, millennials reported an average stress level of 5.4 on a 10-point scale, compared to 4.7 for boomers and 3.7 for matures. Twelve percent of millennials have been diagnosed with an anxiety disorder, compared to eight percent of Gen Xers and seven percent of boomers.[42] And the younger generation may be struggling even more.

Another interesting study found that the amount of vacation workers take has a direct influence on their health and safety,[43] but as we have already learned, we aren't taking as much vacation time as we should.

"One of the Best Years for Facebook ... One of the Worst Years for Me"

"I wish I had lived my life differently," Dustin Moskovitz told a group of high school students not long ago. "I wish I had slept more hours and exercised regularly." Regret and wealth: Moskovitz, a co-founder of Facebook, has both. "2006 was one of the best years for Facebook, and one of the worst years for me as a human," he said.

Despite the fame and wealth that came with starting one of the most iconic new companies in a generation, Moskovitz regrets his work habits from his days at Facebook. He is so passionate on the subject that he gives speeches about the danger of overwork and has written articles about it. He believes he could have been a better leader and a more focused employee. He says, "I would have had fewer panic attacks and acute health problems, like throwing out my back regularly, in my early 20s. I would have been less frustrated and resentful when things went wrong that required me to put in even more hours to deal with a crisis."[44]

Moskovitz is not alone. Tomasz Tunguz, a partner at Redpoint Capital, recalled a complete burnout that ended with a visit to the emergency room when he worked at Google.[45] "I am responsible for setting boundaries. Work time, sleep time, family time, you time," Tunguz said. "If I don't set them properly, things get unbalanced very quickly. Taking time off is essential. Vacations, yes, but also nights and weekends."

Dustin Moskovitz couldn't agree more, saying, "I made a foolish sacrifice on both sides," meaning both his career and his personal life, including his physical and mental health. And despite accumulating wealth, he is adamant that it wasn't worth it for him or for the company. Referring to the cultural tendency toward overwork in tech companies, Moskovitz says, "These companies are both destroying the personal lives of their employees and getting nothing in return."[46]

Moskovitz is putting his ideas into practice as the CEO of Asana, a new productivity software company. He and Asana make company culture and work/life balance core values. Asana recently garnered a rare perfect score from Glassdoor (meaning the company is one of the top companies to work for from an employee perspective), which ranked the company as one of the ten best places to work in 2017.[47] Moskovitz says, "You can do great things AND live your life well. You can have it all, and science says you should."[48]

Sneaking an Email in the Bathroom

Overwork can take a substantial toll on your family, as well. There is one consistent regret that driven, ambitious businesspeople, entrepreneurs, and politicians often mention later in their lives: the sacrifice of their family life. The hours given to work must come from somewhere, and the easiest hours to take are family hours. They will understand, right? After all, aren't you doing this for them? In the short run, there may be no real consequences, but in the long run, the toll can be substantial. These are hours you can't make up.

A friend of mine, who I will call Andy, is an example. As a startup CEO, he had work habits that were brutal. After selling one company, he immediately started a promising new one. I invested, along with a few others. Despite putting in exhausting hours, spending his life savings, and trying in vain for liftoff to a prosperous future, his efforts failed, and he had to shutter the company.

I expected a complete loss from my investment, but to my surprise, he announced a year later that his company's underlying patented technology was being acquired by another company. I was ecstatic for my small investment and for my friend. I ended up making triple my investment, and Andy became rich.

Andy had sacrificed a great deal for his company. I knew of his health issues. Back surgery, migraines, neck problems, mysterious illnesses. I figured he could bounce back from those, even though his health was so shaky that his teenage kids had to help him with menial tasks. But all of that paled in comparison to what became of his family life. A year after the sale, he found out his wife of 20 years was having an affair, and a divorce soon followed. He admitted to me that during the last five to seven years of his startup life, he had been emotionally cold and completely focused on the business, ignoring his wife.

Despite the major success of his two companies, Andy is working to put his life and his body back together. He spends a lot of time in physical therapy, rehabilitating from the damage done by the decade-plus that he ignored his body. Andy is now refocusing on his children, and making sure he spends as much quality time with them as he can to make up for missed time. He is rich, but he doesn't seem happy. And he is not alone. Many people who are successful in business end up severely regretting decisions they made during their careers, and the price tag that came along with them.

"My brightest years running a startup were the darkest ones for my family," said entrepreneur Scott Weiss. The former CEO of IronPort and now managing partner at the powerhouse venture capital firm Andreesen Horowitz, Weiss wrote about his family difficulties in an article on *Medium*.[49] After the sale of his company, Weiss took 18 months off to "reprogram himself." In his new job, he has set boundaries so his family life won't suffer.

In the past, he wrote, "I was often accused of being physically present without being mentally present. (If you find yourself sneaking into the bathroom to complete emails, then you're certainly not in the moment.)" Weiss goes on to say, "When I left IronPort, I realized that committing to my family required disconnecting from work (e.g. turning off the computer and phone), and completely focusing all my attention on the details of the home. Cooking a great meal. Helping with a science project. Discussing the future with my partner."

Weiss calls his new M.O. "disconnect to connect." I call it taking a hard break. But do you have to make a choice between your business on the one hand, and your health and family on the other? Does it have to be one or the other, or is there a better way? A way to enjoy both? I think there is.

CHAPTER 7

A MENTAL HEALTH CRISIS DRIVEN BY TECHNOLOGY

*It has become appallingly obvious that
our technology has exceeded our humanity.*
—ALBERT EINSTEIN

Ever wonder how long the average work email goes unread? Six measly seconds. If ever there was a statistic about how tight a hold technology has on us, that one proves it.[50] Thanks to our phones and the internet, we are on call most of our waking hours, even when we are at home. Communication with work and others in our lives can happen anywhere. While the smartphone liberates people from offices and desks, it also creates a world in which there's no escape or hiding place.

2,617 Times a Day

How many times does the average person touch their phone? 2,617 times a day. The average user spends 2.42 hours a day on their phone. How many times does the average heavy user touch their phone? 5,427 times a day. The average heavy user spends 3.75 hours a day on their phone. The scariest stat is that 87 percent of people surveyed check their phone at least once between midnight and 5:00 a.m.[51] There is a digital leash attached to you wherever you go. And that leash is not good for your mental health.

Think about all the emails and texts we have written—the jokes, serious emails, business highs and lows. Do electronic bits of information weigh anything? Think about phone conversations and voicemails. Do they weigh anything? Of course not, unless you print them out and count the weight of the paper and ink.

Now think about the emotional and psychological weight of our digital lives. It's a whole different story. Don't we need a day when we can shed that weight? Don't we need some time off? Don't our brains and our souls cry out for relief?

A 2015 University of Hamburg study found that extended work availability, or being on call, "has a negative effect: dampening mood and increasing markers of physiological stress." Most notably, the stress carries on into the next day, even when people are no longer on call or working. The most important conclusion of this study was "that the mere prospect of work-related interruptions during free time can exacerbate stress."[52]

Authors of another study found that high job demands over time predicted "emotional exhaustion, psychosomatic complaints, and low work engagement." However, the more psychologically detached people were from work during their off time, the more they buffered themselves from those negative consequences. Taking a hard break from work, when not working, protects people from the negative consequences of being on call.[53]

And it's not just traditional work that we are connected to. We are also connected to every Facebook friend, Twitter follower, Instagram feed, and more. According to one study, the temptation to check the internet "was harder to resist than food or sex."[54] When technology has a more powerful pull than the most basic human needs, we might start to worry.

Would you like to experience more stress than 57 percent of Americans? Then be sure to check your emails and texts on the weekends, and on non-work days. The American Psychological Association (APA) identifies people who do this as "constant checkers." In a survey of Americans' tech-related stress levels, the APA found that 65 percent of respondents acknowledged that taking a "digital detox" is important, but only 28 percent of those actually followed through by turning off and taking a break.[55]

France, a country known for stringent labor laws like the 35-hour workweek, just passed a law that allows workers "the right to disconnect" after leaving work. "These measures are designed to ensure respect for rest periods and...balance between work and family and personal life," a spokesperson for the French ministry of labor said upon passage of the law.[56] My first inclination might be to laugh at another silly French labor law, but is it really so ridiculous?

Some executives in this country aren't waiting for laws like this to be enacted. They are saying enough is enough, and acting. Eileen Carey, CEO of Glassbreakers, a software company building inclusive talent-management technology, went completely dark from social media during the summer of

2016. She calculated that she had been losing four hours a day to Facebook, Instagram, Twitter, and more.[57]

This was difficult, because she had initially built her company through her social media connections. However, once she was past the initial startup phase, those social media bonds grew too wearisome. The return on investment ceased to be there, and the time it took from other activities became excessive. "Shouting into the void does nothing to support and grow a company," she said. And while her action may have been extreme, she was surprised at how productive she was when she was able to focus.

"When the world is shouting through your phone, your desktop, and your Apple Watch, there isn't a lot of time to get insular to carve out the depths of your vision," Carey said. "The most productive self-hack I have ever done was so simple and freeing. I highly encourage all founders to get off social media for at least three months. Your time is your most valuable commodity. You won't believe how much time you'll get back in a day without the distractions of social networks."

Teens Especially at Risk

According to a recent *Atlantic* article, some teenage Snapchat users have sent more than 400,000 "snaps" (messages/photos).[58] Nineteen or twenty thousand "snap" messages is considered a low number for a teen. How do we know? Well, you can just check your Snap score. That's right, it's considered a competition. With school, puberty, popularity, and more, don't teens have enough pressure? Now they're expected to competitively manage their digital lives, as well.

A recent Common Sense Media study revealed that teenagers in 2015 spent nine hours a day wired to technology. Eight- to twelve-year-olds averaged six hours. More importantly, they were often using multiple devices at once and multi-tasking, watching videos while texting and more.[59]

Psychologists are starting to understand the toll this takes on kids, and are seeing that kids don't always love technology. One psychologist notes, "The teens and tweens I've interviewed are often stressed by the feeling that they need to be available at all times. While it's great that they are more connected with their social circles, there's no 'off' once you're in. It can put a lot of pressure on a kid. Unplugged times are effective, and we need to develop other strategies to help students manage social expectations and set realistic expectations for their peers."[60]

During the same period that kids' and teens' use of technology increased steeply, so did their mental health problems. The suicide rate for U.S. middle school students doubled from 2007 to 2014, and death by suicide now surpasses death in car crashes for those aged 10 to 14, according to the Centers for Disease Control.[61] Experts are flummoxed. A frightening article in *San Francisco Magazine* discussed the problem of suicide not as it applies to Silicon Valley entrepreneurs, but to children living in Palo Alto.[62]

Health clinics on college campuses are flooded with mental health issues. [63] In the past five years, Ohio State has seen a 43 percent jump in the number of students being treated at the university's counseling center. At the University of Central Florida in Orlando, the increase has been about 12 percent each year over the past decade. At the University of Michigan in Ann Arbor, demand for counseling-center services has increased by 36 percent in the last seven years. Seventeen percent of college students were diagnosed with or treated for anxiety problems during the past year, *The Wall Street Journal* reported. That is an astonishing number.

Jean Twenge, a professor of psychology at San Diego State University, corroborates the decline in teen mental health in an article for *The Washington Post*.[64] Twenge points to national data showing that the number of American teens suffering from depression surged by 33 percent between 2010 and 2015, and during that time the number of suicides among 13- to 18-year-olds increased by 31 percent. She points out that smartphone use by teens also grew dramatically during that same period: by 2012, more than 50 percent of teens had smartphones, and by 2015, that number was 73 percent.

Given that other mental-health risk factors—economic or academic pressure, for example—were stable or decreasing during that period, Twenge sees a high likelihood that the surge in smartphone use caused the surge in depression and suicide. Data has also shown that "teens who spent five or more hours a day online were 71 percent more likely than those who spent only one hour a day to have at least one suicide risk factor (depression, thinking about suicide, making a suicide plan, or attempting suicide). Overall, suicide risk factors rose significantly after two or more hours a day online."

Those are sobering facts. Also sobering is how some social media executives who helped create the ubiquitous technology are now viewing their creations. They are coming out publicly to apologize for their role in the deterioration of culture, and to warn others to be careful about how they use the products they've made. Two prominent former Facebook executives in particular have recently made remarks to this effect. Facebook's founding president, Sean Parker, said:

The thought process that went into building these applications... was all about: "How do we consume as much of your time and conscious attention as possible?" And that means that we need to sort of give you a little dopamine hit every once in a while, because someone liked or commented on a photo or a post or whatever...It's a social-validation feedback loop...exactly the kind of thing that a hacker like myself would come up with, because you're exploiting a vulnerability in human psychology.

He added, ominously, "God only knows what it's doing to our children's brains."[65]

Chamath Palihapitiya, the former VP of user growth at Facebook and now a prominent venture capitalist at the firm Social Capital, recently described social media this way to an audience at Stanford University: "If you feed the beast, that beast will destroy you. If you push back on it, we have a chance to control it. People need to hard break from some of these tools and things you rely on." Amazingly, he told the crowd that he does not allow his own children to use social media—at all.[66] This from the guy who used to drive user growth at Facebook!

Whether you are a child or teenager, a CEO, a middle manager, a doctor, or a postal worker, the message is clear: your sanity depends on your taking time on a regular basis to unplug.

Take My Phone—Please!
Digital Detox is a company that has led retreats focused on meditation, yoga, and one-on-one connections for more than 1,200 participants, including executives from Apple, Intel, Google, Airbnb, Pandora, and TOMS Shoes.

They have a strict policy against the use of technology. Levi Felix is the creator of Digital Detox. When he was 24 years old, Felix was flying high. He was the vice president of a thriving startup, living the tech dream. He was also working harsh hours. Before he knew it, he was in the hospital, having lost a lot of blood due to an esophageal tear. He was completely and utterly burned out and exhausted. Shocked at his sudden loss of health, Felix stepped off the fast-moving train he was on, packed a backpack, and traveled around the world. His journey included a ten-day silent retreat, and living for a time on a remote island in Cambodia. He came back a changed man, and wanted to spread the lessons he had learned.

In addition to Digital Detox, Felix created Camp Grounded, an adult summer camp where people put their digital devices in "biohazard" bags at the beginning of their stay and then enjoy friendly activities such archery, capture the flag, singing songs, and more. The goal is to help people break their addiction to their digital devices.[67]

Felix clearly tapped into the zeitgeist. Think of the popularity of Burning Man, an annual festival in the desert 120 miles north of Reno, Nevada. Burning Man is especially favored by those in the tech industry, who go to escape the very thing they created, connect to nature, and build things with their hands. There are also $1,000-a-night resorts in the Caribbean where no phones exist or will work. Hotel guests have to use flags on a flagpole to communicate with the management.[68]

We have to ask what is going on when people are willing to pay to escape the digital world and have someone else force them to stop using their technology. Seth Godin, prominent author and entrepreneur, writes that your phone is using you. He says, "Your smartphone has two jobs. On one hand, it was hired by you to accomplish certain tasks. In the overall scheme of things, it's a screaming bargain and a miracle." He adds, "But most of the time, your phone holds you hostage to corporations, assorted acquaintances and large social networks. They've hired it to put you to work for them. You're not the customer, you're the product. Your attention and your anxiety is getting sold, cheap. When your phone grabs your attention, when it makes you feel inadequate, when it pushes you to catch up, to consume and to fret... it's not really working for you, is it?"[69]

In other words, your smartphone's second job is to grab your attention. And it is addicting. I know, because I am just as addicted to my smartphone and other devices as the next person. But I advocate that we all make an effort to relearn how to be together and connect with each other without the aid of devices.

In 2009, Stefan Teodosic, executive director of Beber Camp, a Jewish summer camp for kids ages seven to 17, instituted a screen-free policy, to the howls of many campers and a couple of irate parents. The first few days were rougher than normal, because some campers sneaked in the electronic devices, only to have them confiscated. But the camp staff soon started to notice real changes in the interactions of the kids, who began connecting on a much deeper level, as Teodosic was surprised to discover.

The key moment came when Teodosic was approached by a small group of 15-year-old boys who had been coming to the camp for a few years. Expecting an argument, he was shocked when the kids thanked him for the screen-free policy, saying that they had never been closer to each other and had experienced better conversations and connections than at any time in their previous camp experience. They left the stunned executive director with high fives. The camp has been screen-free ever since, and now no one argues or has a problem with the policy.[70] In my conversations with Teodosic, he could not be prouder of his camp as a leader in the screen-free camp movement. Other camps have followed with similar policies.

Levi Felix would be pleased to hear that his message is spreading to youth camps. Unfortunately, Felix was diagnosed with brain cancer and died in 2017. David Cygielman, CEO of the Moishe House Foundation, said, "Levi lived more in his short life than most people do in their entire life." The insight that he communicated to thousands of people was that we need a break; we need to escape and step away from the fast-paced and frenetic world we live in.

CHAPTER 8

SHINING A LIGHT ON DEPRESSION

*Knowing your own darkness is the best method for dealing with
the darknesses of other people.*

—CARL JUNG

One serial entrepreneur was recently quoted as saying, "I think if you're signing up to start something... you're signing up to burn out... that's just part of the deal."[71] Brad Feld used to be one of those burned-out people. An MIT graduate, he built and sold his first company at age 24. That was the beginning of a storied career as a venture capitalist that included co-founding Mobius Venture Capital and Intensity Ventures. He is co-founder of Techstars, a mentor-driven startup accelerator that is considered one of the best in the world. Through coaching, insight, and fundraising, this program helps companies and entrepreneurs accelerate growth and succeed.

His most recent venture firm is Foundry Group, which he co-founded. It has raised over $1 billion to invest in startups. Their investments include FitBit and Zynga, as well as many other companies that have been acquired by Google and Twitter. In addition to managing his highly successful business career, Brad is quite active in the nonprofit world, contributes to several widely read blogs, and is an avid long-distance runner who has completed 23 marathons.

While Brad Feld is everything you would expect in a hard-charging, red-blooded venture capitalist, he also suffers from depression and has had suicidal thoughts in the past. Feld has taken numerous steps to deal with depression, anxiety, and the pressures of work in the startup world. "I can work until I hit a wall. The problem is not necessarily the hitting of the wall, but that recovering after hitting the wall takes so much time," he told me. "I used to be the guy who got up at 5:00 a.m., no matter what time zone I was in."

The Specter of Suicide in Workaholic Cultures

Suicide and depression are the dark secrets of the Silicon Valley startup culture. Everyone likes to follow Mark Zuckerberg's success with Facebook, or Larry Page and Sergey Brin and their triumphs with Google. But how many of you have heard of Jody Sherman, Ilya Zhitomirskiy, Aaron Swartz, Austen Heinz, Faigy Mayer, or Matt Berman? They are just a few of the higher-profile founders of tech startups who have committed suicide in recent years.

Failure can seem overwhelming. When you feel that failure defines you, you are a failure, and there may seem to be only one way out. This is apparently what happened to Jody Sherman, the founder of Ecomom, an eco-friendly e-commerce site. The company burned through money and did not have the capital to sustain itself. Two weeks before the company went under, Jody Sherman shot himself in his parked car.

A recent article in an online business publication profiled new startups whose mission is to deliver pills and drinks that will let you be productive for up to 16 hours a day.[72] This is exactly the kind of thinking that leads to mental breakdowns. A study of British civil servants found that people who worked more than 11 hours a day, compared to those who worked only seven to eight hours a day, "were more than twice as likely to have a major depressive episode, even when they had no previous mental health issues."[73]

According to Dr. Michael Freeman, a clinical professor at the University of California, San Francisco, 49 percent of the 242 entrepreneurs he surveyed reported mental health conditions such as depression, ADHD, or anxiety.[74] Depression was the most common condition, at 30 percent. Consider that the national average for depression is only seven percent. There are two likely reasons for such a huge discrepancy. One is that the people who start companies are often idiosyncratic individuals who have mental health issues to begin with. The other is that after founding and running a company, they develop mental health problems. It is likely some of both.

The stress and mental trauma of bringing a company to life, along with the roller coaster ride of survival and success, exacts a heavy price. When you found a company, you are the face of that company, and you may feel that you *are* the company. When your company is dying, it can feel like your identity is dying along with it. With no break, no perspective, and nothing else but your company, you could be in a very toxic mindset without even knowing it.

This isn't just a problem in tech. From 1999 to 2012, the percentage of Americans on antidepressants almost doubled, from 6.8 percent to 13 percent.[75] (Curious that the use of antidepressants is almost double the reported national average for depression itself. It could be that depression, or its symptoms, are more common than reports indicate.) Besides startups, one other epicenter of the culture of overwork is finance.

In early 2015, Sarvshreshth Gupta was exhausted. He told his father about his new job at Goldman Sachs: "This job is not for me. Too much work and too little time." The 22-year-old Wharton School graduate was tired after pulling all-nighters and 100-hour workweeks. On April 16, 2015, he jumped to his death from his apartment building. Twenty-nine-year-old Thomas Hughes, who worked at the boutique investment firm Moelis & Company, jumped from his luxury apartment in May 2015.[76]

It would be hard to find places in America where working 24/7 is more highly prized than the worlds of startups and finance. Both lionize burning the proverbial midnight oil. Driven individuals in these centers of innovation and finance seem to push each other to work more and more. As we've said, a lot of that ethos is about signaling behavior and machismo, not the actual quality of the work being done or the decisions being made. Who can work the hardest? Who is toughest, and who will sacrifice the most? Not: who is doing the best work possible?

Some big Wall Street firms have sensed that something is very wrong, and they're trying to make changes. In 2016, J.P. Morgan initiated a new "Pencils Down" policy. The new policy, announced on an internal phone call, is to encourage the company's investment bankers to take weekends off. However, there is a big exception: "...as long as there isn't a live deal in the works." The firm's head of global banking, Carlos Hernandez, was quoted as saying that the policy is designed to get people out of the office and back home, or wherever they choose to relax. This builds upon a policy

J.P. Morgan instituted a few years earlier that allows employees to flag a "protected weekend" for events like a college reunion or wedding.[77]

Since 2014, Bank of America has encouraged junior staffers to take off at least four weekend days a month, according to *The Wall Street Journal*. Goldman Sachs is also trying to change, requiring its analysts take Saturdays off. But it remains to be seen how serious any of these companies are about changing their culture. If they just write these policies into employee handbooks, but don't enforce them, the policies will be ignored.

Sarvshreshth Gupta's father was quoted in *The New York Times* as saying that the last time he and his son spoke, his son said to him, "I have not slept in two days, I have to complete a presentation for a client meeting in the morning, my VP is annoyed, and I am working alone in my office." This kind of behavior is highly destructive, and it needs to change. Magnifying the tragedy of these suicides is all the data we've presented that clearly shows how unproductive overwork is. With suicide rates at a 30-year high in the U.S.,[78] we should start focusing on the tools we have to fix this problem, such as disconnecting and taking breaks from work. With all the research showing correlations between overwork, "constant checking," and poor mental health, I suspect we could save a lot of lives.

A Digital Sabbath

Brad Feld is trying to shine a light on mental health problems in the startup world. Not only is he giving talks about his personal issues, he is also setting an example. For 16 years, Feld took one week off each quarter to completely disconnect from work, email, and phones. This, however, did not prove to be enough. In a conversation with Feld, he told me that in 2012, he suffered an episode of depression and exhaustion so intense that he spent the next six months sleeping upward of 11 hours a night. This was a stark signal to him that he needed more than a one-week break every three months.

So, in early 2013, Feld implemented a digital Sabbath. Now he does not work from Friday night through Saturday night, and sometimes Sunday morning. "I felt boxed in by calendar and commitments," Feld said, "and now, I give myself space. Now I don't hit the wall." He said the weekly break "allows me to maintain an intense pace of work." He makes a comparison to long-distance running, saying, "You simply don't do as well if you over-train."

"I wish I had re-evaluated my work rhythm earlier in my life," Feld said. "A lot of my personality and self-worth was tied up in how I was working, and it really wasn't healthy or enjoyable for me over the past 30 years. I wish I had spent more time re-evaluating my work habits." This is a refrain I've heard from many successful people across a number of different industries.

Feld famously sets his out-of-office email to tell people: "I am on sabbatical. I will not be reading this email. When I return, I'm archiving everything and starting with an empty inbox...If you want me to see it, please send it again after August 12th."

Feld told me that he is no longer a slave to the information coming at him. He has more time and space to think and reflect. And he feels that the quality of his work and his insights are significantly better. He noted that time away increases his interest in the work he is doing rather than causing him to feel boxed in. On the personal side, he said, "The person I want to spend most of my time with is my wife. I'm very present and engaged." He loves that every week, he has little in the way of distractions from her.

For Feld, a digital Sabbath is the best of all worlds: his work is much better, he is more engaged and less likely to burn out, he is less likely to become depressed, and he gets more quality time with his wife and friends. There is a powerful lesson in the changes Brad Feld has made in his life, and the benefits those changes have brought to his work life, his mental health, and his marriage: in order to thrive, we need to build a hard break into our lives.

PART TWO

THE VALUE OF A HARD BREAK

CHAPTER 9

A PALACE IN TIME

The seventh day is a palace in time which we build.

—ABRAHAM JOSHUA HESCHEL

Cut back to me in July of 2003, crying in the shower. Like Brad Feld, I knew I had to make some important changes. After much reflection, I realized that a waking life that was 97 to 99 percent business and one to three percent everything else was simply not good for my health. So, in July 2003, I went back to my initial line of thinking, and decided to join the synagogue in Atlanta where I had gone to services. I was dejected to find that the rabbi I had felt such a connection with had retired from being the pulpit rabbi for over 30 years, and had been replaced by a different rabbi.

The Unexpected Rabbi

My frustration led me to believe that I needed to start anew in a different location. In Atlanta, I was managing $5 million of other people's money, and had only myself as an employee. I had no family to support, and I could work anywhere. All I needed was a phone and a computer. So why not try someplace new?

I made a list of everything I wanted in a place to live. I did not want a big city. I wanted there to be no excuse not to go outside and exercise. I wanted a solid Jewish community that I could join, and I dreamed of being near the water. With no connections to hold me back, I could live anywhere within reason. Charleston, South Carolina, was one option. The small towns north of San Diego were another. One intriguing possibility was Santa Barbara, California. I had visited there once, and it seemed great, but I didn't know anyone who lived there.

In December of 2003, I ended up flying out to Santa Barbara on a whim. Santa Barbara, if you have never been, is a beautiful place, but I knew no one, and I felt very lonely. I had flown in on a Thursday, and the next day my brother called to see how my trip was going. He asked if I was going to Friday-night Shabbat services. I laughed and asked why he was asking me about services, when he never went himself. Then I stopped and thought that if I really wanted to change my life and join a community, this would be one way to do it.

Imagine my surprise when after sitting down for services, out walked the rabbi who had retired from the Atlanta synagogue—the one with whom I had felt such a strong connection. I was stunned. After services, I introduced myself to Rabbi Alvin Sugarman. He thought my story was one of the funniest things he had ever heard, and proceeded to introduce me to every single person at the reception that followed.

Taking this as a sign, I moved to Santa Barbara three months later, in March of 2004, knowing only Rabbi Sugarman. That move changed my life. I started to develop a life outside of work. I regularly got outdoors, and I became a member of the real community fostered by the synagogue.

Then a surprising thing happened—well, maybe not so surprising. My investment returns started to rebound, and my business began doing well again. This was the first time I had realized the power of my mindset to influence my work, and I finally understood that doing more work did not necessarily improve my performance. In fact, doing too much work could harm it.

Something pulled at me, and I decided to try to understand Judaism a little more deeply. Once I started studying its rich history, I realized that Judaism is really one big discussion and argument about how to live a good, meaningful life. For over 2,000 years, rabbis, scholars, and regular people have been arguing and wrestling with the questions "What is a good life?" and "What is a meaningful life?"

During my early career in business and investing, I made at least a cursory attempt at the good life by taking one vacation a year, for a week or two. During that vacation, I really attempted to disconnect, refresh, and regenerate myself. And it worked...for about a month. A month into my nonstop work routine, I would find myself facing the same mental exhaustion. In the back of my mind, I knew there had to be a way to regularly recharge myself without having to disappear to some remote location.

Baby Steps Toward Sabbath

As I got deeper into the study of Judaism—which enriched my life in ways I could never have imagined—an answer to the question of how to regularly recharge began to emerge from within the Jewish tradition: it's called Shabbat. Shabbat is the Hebrew word for Sabbath. In the Jewish tradition of Shabbat, one is not permitted to do any work from nightfall on Friday until nightfall on Saturday. This time is meant to be spent resting, being with family, reconnecting with friends, and praying. The idea of completely shutting off business and work was so foreign and exotic that it truly enticed me. I wondered how I could implement the antiquated concept of a day of complete rest and no business in the modern, 24/7 digital world.

In the summer of 2005, I decided to make a change and begin to implement a Sabbath in my life. It is significant that I realized I needed to change my life in the summer of 2003, but did not fully act on it for two more years! Change and commitment are truly hard. And even when I made that decision, I wasn't ready to do it all overnight. My initial decision was to turn off my cell phone and computer right before bedtime on Friday night, and to force myself to keep them off until noon on Saturday. Some people in the Jewish tradition define the pause in "work" as not only a pause in conducting business, but also a pause in driving, using electricity, or using money for any purpose (among other restrictions). For me, the Jewish tradition of the Sabbath was a guideline, and really an excuse to try and force myself to step back from my worst habits and take a break from my business. I decided I would still go out with friends during Sabbath, attend live sports events, watch movies, and drive a car. But I would not talk about or focus on business.

Back in 2005, I had a BlackBerry; and while it was not as powerful as my current iPhone, it allowed me unprecedented access to the internet, email, and communication with others. To someone who is as curious as I am, the internet, and especially a smartphone, is a double-edged sword. On the one hand, these incredible devices put endless amounts of information at my fingertips. On the other hand, there is always something more to learn or discover, and it is easy to get lost in browsing, reading, planning, and working without ever coming up for air. There is always more research to do, some new investment to learn about; there are interesting people to talk to, and unlimited things to read and understand. It never ends.

When I started my Sabbath experiment, I was so attuned to the buzzing, blinking, and ringing of my BlackBerry, I was a Pavlovian dog salivating every time it made a sound. That very first time I turned off my phone and computer from Friday evening till noon on Saturday was really hard. I wondered what I was missing. I wondered if family or friends were trying to reach me. Nevertheless, I made it through Friday night and four or five hours on Saturday morning without turning on my phone. I survived the experiment.

After a few weeks, I decided to see if I could make it to 3:00 p.m. on Saturday. It really wasn't much harder than waiting until noon. I could do it. After a few months, I realized that I could make it through an entire 24-hour period, and I started completely shutting down from sunset to sunset, as is the custom in Judaism.

Benefits Expected and Unexpected

I didn't know it then, but this weekly change in my behavior would have many very positive results in my personal and business life.

By resting one day a week and completely shutting off work, I saw a clear reduction in my stress and anxiety levels. It took several weeks for me to realize that I had a weekly opportunity to relax. I didn't have to disappear for long vacations. I had a vacation every week! Just catching up on sleep, not having an alarm or a hard-and-fast schedule, felt liberating. Simply put, what I experienced when I turned off my phone and computer and gave myself a day of rest was freedom.

There are few things I love more than sleeping in. Before I became a father, I always looked forward to sleeping in on the Sabbath. Once I had my daughter, I could no longer sleep in, so I began taking a nap when she did. Just the act of sleeping a little bit more made me feel like a king. Frankly, it feels like a gift from heaven. What better way is there to truly relax and refresh yourself than to take a nap? And I could enjoy this extra sleep, because I wasn't worried about working.

It is ironic that the act of restriction frees us. Senator Joseph Lieberman, a devout orthodox Jew, says in his book *The Gift of Rest* that the Jewish Sabbath law has this way of setting us free.[79] Many people get that feeling from stepping outside their normal routines and patterns.

Do you ever wonder why a vacation at a hotel feels so good? Sure, someone cleans your room and cooks your meals, but there is something more. After all, you could hire a cleaning service and go out to dinner at home, so what is the big difference when you're on vacation? I believe it lies in feeling that the demands of our daily routines have been lifted. Vacation feels great because we are temporarily free from responsibility. And that feels amazing. Unfortunately, you have to pay for vacations with hard-earned money. The fantastic part about the Sabbath is that it's absolutely free! You get the same freedom from work without the cost.

Can you visualize allowing your load of responsibilities and worries to simply subside for one day a week? While I try not to think about business or investments during the Sabbath, ideas invariably pop into my head. Connections form that help my understanding of what has happened in the past six days, and what the next six might bring. This is how our minds work. Once you relax, insights are suddenly easier to form. (I will return to this idea in Chapter 14: This Is Your Brain on Downtime.)

Having the time to spend with family, friends, my wife, and my children is priceless. And it is a different kind of time. There are no competing interests from my business, and no digital interruptions. I can simply hang out, have meaningful conversations, and take it slow. In his seminal book, *The Sabbath*, the great Rabbi Abraham Joshua Heschel called the Sabbath a "palace in time." That is truly how it feels to me: regal, privileged, rich.

An unexpected benefit of my weekly ritual of unplugging is the excitement I feel when I do plug back in. Before I made the commitment to a 24/6 lifestyle, I hoped that taking a day of rest would be a great source of stress relief and refreshment, but I did not realize how enjoyable it would be to return to the business world each week.

The Sabbath is a wonderful way to fight burnout. By pausing every week, you get the chance to become excited by what you may have missed: emails, conversations, project updates, phone calls, business opportunities, and more. I find myself renewed and ready for the fight every week, and more importantly, I have renewed interest in taking on that week's challenges.

Little did I know that when I started taking a day off, I would be on the road to becoming a much stronger and more resilient person, both in business and in life. The routine of weekly work with a guaranteed day of rest allows me to endure the hours of toil in a more graceful and energetic way. It is allowing me to work harder over the long term, because I have a built-in buffer that protects me from burning out.

Over the years, the Sabbath prepared me for the biggest roller coaster ride I have ever been on—The American Home Real Estate Company.

CHAPTER 10

THE WILD RIDE OF MY STARTUP, THE AMERICAN HOME

If somebody offers you an amazing opportunity but you are not sure you can do it, say yes—then learn how to do it later!

—RICHARD BRANSON

In early 2008, I was still living in Santa Barbara when a close friend asked me to partner with him in the purchase of a rental home in Charlotte, North Carolina. I had never owned a home before, and was happy to be renting as the housing and foreclosure crisis exploded across the country. My friend was the founder of a successful nonprofit who wanted to find a way to build long-term wealth. Like most other professional money managers and investors, I was grappling with how to protect my investors' capital against the greatest financial crisis since the Great Depression. Several of my investors were panicking.

It was a challenging time for everyone but I was not only able to be calm in the face of the crisis, I started looking for opportunity. Why was I more resilient now than before, when a minor speed bump had caused my mental health to career off the tracks? I credit my foundation of Judaism, the Sabbath, and having a healthy personal life outside of business. All of those took years to develop.

My close friend was mistrustful of the stock market, especially when the financial crisis hit and the stock market cratered. He had reached out to trusted advisors who recommended investing in real estate, specifically investment rental properties. After much research, he found that he could buy rental houses and make a bit more in rent than the cost of a mortgage in Charlotte, North Carolina, a growing southern city with long-term positive demographic trends. He had already partnered with a few other investors and acquired about a dozen homes. And now he approached me, and asked if I was interested.

What did I know about houses? Not much. But I did know what constituted a good investment. By this time, I had been building my investment management company for ten years. I had grown a $1 million initial investment into more than $25 million in assets at its peak. I had an assistant, a real office, and a full-time analyst. This was when my friend approached me.

From Hedge Funds to Houses

Together, we purchased four homes in Charlotte. One was a four-bedroom, two-bath home that cost $75,000. We invested $10,000 in repairs and rented the home for $1,000 a month. I thought, "This is pretty good; there is no way you could build a house for $85,000." The fact that you'd have to spend a lot more to build a house than what we'd paid for it meant that we'd gotten the home at well below replacement cost. The home provided a 14 percent annual gross return on rental income over your initial investment. Net of annual expenses such as insurance, taxes, and maintenance, this gross return would mean a seven-to-eight-percent annual net return. Add in some debt financing, and we could easily earn double-digit returns with little apparent risk. I told a few other people about this opportunity, including investors in my hedge fund. Several asked how could they take part.

In 2009, I launched a small partnership called the Sabre Value Queen City Fund (Charlotte is known as the Queen City, after Queen Charlotte). I convinced my analyst—a talented, smart, and driven woman—to move from Santa Barbara to Charlotte to buy homes for me. (She is now a very successful real estate agent with 15 other agents working for her.)

Back in 2009, when I said I was investing in homes, most people looked at me as if I had a third eye on my forehead. Who in their right mind would buy houses in this market? Furthermore, they wondered, why would I launch a $1.3 million fund that only owned 16 homes? Many investors and colleagues didn't understand why I would go through the effort to start a new business for such a small amount of money. I thought there was a possibility that this would become a real business one day, or that maybe it would be a sleepy little investment that would take ten years to pay off.

What started out as a small partnership grew quickly when one investor asked if I could create a partnership just for him. This investor was the CEO of a very successful money-management firm and would become a valued mentor, as he had experience in startups (he was one of the first few investors in a small company called Amazon).

Two years later, in 2011, I was running two businesses: a hedge fund that was slowly but surely recovering from the financial crisis, and a fledging single-family home rental business with about 150 homes in Charlotte. I was making mistakes, but the business was cash-flow-positive. I started paying small dividends to investors as our rental revenue exceeded our expenses. And there was a seemingly endless supply of homes to buy.

Around that time, my personal life was changing, as well. In February of 2009, in my ongoing quest to educate myself about Judaism, I traveled to Los Angeles for a Jewish learning retreat. That was where I met Valerie, who is now my wife. It didn't take me long to realize how incredible she was. February 2009 was a very rough time for financial markets, my hedge fund, and my own personal wealth and fortune. If I had not already been working on my inner life and strengthening my own capabilities, I'm sure I would have missed the opportunity to meet my wife, and the fact that I could be open to love at this extremely challenging time for me professionally demonstrated how much bandwidth my inner work and my commitment to the Sabbath had given me, especially as compared to what I had been capable of in 2003.

Only 18 months after our first date, Valerie and I were married. Valerie wanted to study public health with a focus on nutrition, and was accepted to graduate programs at both UCLA and Emory University. We decided that Emory was a better fit for her, and since I could work anywhere—and my small, but growing home rental business was in nearby Charlotte—we moved to Atlanta in August 2010. I have moved many times during my life, and this was my third move to Atlanta.

A few months later, after we had settled, I took a tour of the city with a real estate agent. I could not believe the scale of the foreclosure problem there. Atlanta had been especially hard-hit by the housing crisis. It was only then, in 2011, that I realized the enormity of the problem.

I began touring empty foreclosed homes by the hundreds with real estate agents in neighborhood after neighborhood. Overgrown lawns and boarded-up windows were just two signs. Inside some of the homes, I saw heartbreaking signs of the upheaval in the lives of the people who'd lived in them, such as a young child's handwriting on the wall saying goodbye to her house.

Who was going to fix up these empty homes? Who was going to renovate and bring the capital to bear to revitalize neighborhoods? Not only did I see the investment opportunity, I felt a calling to help rebuild homes and neighborhoods, and bring desperately-needed capital and jobs back to the housing market.

For a few years, it felt like I was the only one crazy enough to be doing this. I spoke with several investors about growing the real estate portion of my business. The original investor in my hedge fund came out for a tour, and immediately saw the scale of the opportunity. No strangers to opportunity, he and his father had built and sold a student loan company, then taken the proceeds and started another student loan company that eventually originated and securitized over $9 billion in loans.

We agreed to a partnership, creating a business that could grow to manage many more than the 150 homes we currently had. More importantly, since I had no experience running an operating company, he committed to helping me recruit a C-level executive suite. While my friend and his colleagues were working to operationalize the company, I would be CEO and focus on acquisitions, strategy, and growth. We renamed the company The American Home, and got to work. By early 2012, we had about 250 homes and eight employees. We decided to launch a partnership to raise $25 million. I ended up raising $100 million in only three months. That was when everything changed.

The Wild Ride Begins

Exponential growth was not something I was prepared for. In 2012 alone, The American Home (TAH) grew ten times in terms of the number of homes owned, employee count, and capital. We started the year with around 200 homes and ended with 2,000; eight employees grew to more than 100; and $25 million in capital became $200 million. By the end of 2012, we were meeting with investment banks about taking the company public. A company that had barely existed the year before was suddenly being pitched to be traded on Wall Street.

We bought each home individually, one by one. At one point in 2012, we were buying homes at a rate of ten a day. To acquire that many homes, we had to make offers on thousands. I built a team of four analysts, and had dozens of people in the field. Only a year before, the whole company had consisted of me and two additional employees. Our teams visited each home to assess its state of repair and estimate how much would have to be spent on fixing it up.

In addition to buying homes that were listed on the market, we participated in monthly auctions at county courthouses. In Georgia, auctions are held the first Tuesday of each month on the county courthouse steps. The problem was that there are 159 different counties in Georgia. Depending on who you ask, anywhere from 10 to 20 counties make up the massive Greater Atlanta area. Some of our houses were 80 miles apart, but still considered to be in some part of Atlanta. Coordinating field visits to homes before making offers was one thing, but participating in 10 to 20 different auctions at the same time—without making costly mistakes—was another. We needed bodies at these auctions, and often enlisted friends and family (including my wife, Valerie) to go and bid on houses for us.

In July 2012, two giant investment firms, Colony Capital and Blackstone, entered the market to buy foreclosed homes. Previously, TAH had the market to itself, but now the competition became fierce. It was a giant land grab before the pipeline of foreclosed houses disappeared. We moved fast to make more and more offers, expanding into Orlando, Tampa, and Nashville. Growth was exhilarating. We had to move offices twice after running out of room. I remember at one point it was so cramped that four people were working out of a single 100-square-foot office. That was probably not up to code, but we were all too busy and excited to notice. By the end of 2012, we were flying high, and had merged all our partnerships into one REIT (real estate investment trust) structure to prepare the company to go to the next level.

If you've never been a part of a startup, or experienced a company growing exponentially, it is hard to understand the level of buzz and excitement, and sometimes sheer panic, that pervaded TAH. Our head of technology described it as trying to change the tire on a moving car. In a similar vein, LinkedIn founder Reid Hoffman famously said, "In founding a startup, you throw yourself off a cliff and build an airplane on the way down."

In late 2012, with the company seemingly ready to take off, the board and I started discussions about bringing in a new CEO. We talked about finding someone with Wall Street experience who could lead the company, do quarterly earnings calls, and take the whole thing to another level. While I had built the company from 16 homes to 2,000, maybe it was time to pass the baton on to someone who could take it to the tens of thousands. We started conversations with a CEO who ran a publicly-traded REIT and actively tried to recruit him, but the board ultimately decided he would be too expensive and wasn't the right fit.

And we had other problems...big problems. Our operations were struggling, especially in scaling up to handle the volume of homes. While we were buying 200 to 300 homes a month, we were repairing only 50 to 75, and renting about 50. In January of 2013, we owned 2,000 homes and had 500 more under contract, but only 500 of our homes were rented. We had a huge backlog of empty homes, and empty homes invite problems like vandalism, theft, mold, and pest infestation. Empty homes cost money in terms of taxes, insurance, lawn maintenance, etc.—and they don't generate revenue. The board stopped its CEO search when they realized the depth of our operational problems.

In January 2013, we recognized that we couldn't change the tire on a moving car, so we made a pit stop: we decided to halt acquisitions and direct the entire company to work on fixing operations. We had 18 different locations where we stored data in multiple forms, from Excel spreadsheets to expensive database software. We realized that we had multiple people "walking a home" (going through and making sure all repairs and renovations were done and all the fixtures worked, so the place would be ready for a family to move into) for a total of about a dozen different times before each home became rent-ready. Our property management group was not collaborating sufficiently with the rehab division in order to ensure smooth transitions. Additionally, our call center was overwhelmed, and not structured efficiently to handle all the incoming leasing and maintenance calls.

As people worked around the clock to fix processes, repair homes, and get them rented, I began to see the real effects of working without taking a break. TAH employees were burning out. Bad decisions and mistakes that had been chalked up to hyper-growth could no longer be overlooked. Simmering inter-office politics began boiling over everywhere. Rehab and repair blamed property management for a variety of issues, and vice versa. The problems weren't caused by lack of effort. On the contrary, people were working *too* hard, and therefore not always working effectively or making good decisions. Everyone was exhausted, and I had been so focused on growing the company and staying ahead of competitors that I did not realize the damage being done.

Adding to the stress, we were also engaged in a daily fight for cash. In my rush to buy as many homes as possible, I had committed to more purchases than we had money to pay for. To make matters worse, the company was losing money every month due to its huge workforce and insufficient number of rented homes. I cannot describe how unbelievably stressful it is to maintain a positive outlook for investors and employees, while struggling with dys-functional operations and worrying every day if we would run out of cash.

While we did make progress on the operations and on bringing down our cash flow drain through the spring and summer of 2013, it became clear that the company needed a complete overhaul. We restructured in August. Except for me, the entire management team changed, and we went from 180 employees back down to 80 in six months. Firing people is awful. There is no good way to do it, but I tried to lead with compassion. We gave generous severance packages when we could, and helped with job placement.

I Just Happened to Have a Baby Strapped to My Chest

Leading a company full of employees worried about their jobs and investors worried about their investments was a very difficult endeavor. The feeling of letting everyone down became overwhelming, at times. This led to sleepless nights, a general feeling of being run down, and what I will call, for the sake of politeness, "intestinal distress." For someone who had never had more than two employees and zero operational experience, I was getting the education of a lifetime—but not the one I wanted.

When the dust settled on TAH after our August 2013 restructuring, I found myself asking some big questions. What did we get out of all the long hours? Did people make better decisions? Were they more productive? Was the company better off for all this work?

Once I asked the questions, I started noticing something interesting. In general, the people who talked the most about working hard were the least effective employees. One executive in particular, by all outward appearances, was one of the hardest workers in our company. He always bragged about working the "third shift," which meant after midnight. And this executive drove the people underneath him hard.

Up until the restructuring, we had been growing so fast that we just assumed all of his long hours, emails, and talk of hard work added up to something. Unfortunately, we discovered that he was completely disorganized, and his work quality was awful. His long hours and management style were hurting the company. It was shocking to discover that behind the wizard's curtain, those long hours were hiding terrible work habits and processes as well as disorganization. That was when I realized that sending emails at two in the morning was not something to be proud of, or to be rewarded.

More proof of the fact that overwork is unlikely to improve results could be found in the countless presentations we put together for our board. In hindsight (which, of course, is always 20/20), we delayed key decisions for months as we prepared presentation after presentation and performed analysis after analysis, instead of diving right into problems and fixing them. Instead of analyzing for the board, we simply needed to roll up our sleeves and rebuild the company from the ground up. Many of our processes and communications (and the overall way our company was functioning) were not sound. Analysis paralysis drove a lot of unnecessary work and a lot of long hours that now seemed wasted—those hours of work could have been focused on things like how customer service calls were taken and responded to, how to avoid evictions, and how to lower turnover and increase renewals. I attribute these errors to not enough pausing and reflecting. Instead, we were caught up in the disease of busyness, focused on pleasing investors, and just plain weary from overwork.

My life raft through this whole experience was the 24-hour "palace in time" I entered every week from sundown Friday to sundown Saturday. If I hadn't observed the Sabbath and taken one day a week away from work, I never would have made it through. I would have burned out, quit, or worse, been fired by irate investors and an angry board of directors. I would not have had the fortitude and resilience to endure the ups and downs of such an intense experience, especially in 2013, when most days felt like failures. Contrast this to 2003, when simply having a portfolio down five percent felt like the end of the world.

How can one enjoy a better work/life balance? That seems to be the million-dollar question these days. I smile when I hear people ask this question, or when the topic emerges in conversation or in an article I'm reading. I truly believe it is the wrong question. I don't think it is possible to have a work/life balance, because I don't think there is such a thing. Or, if such a balance exists, it is extremely difficult to pull off in today's business world. It was certainly impossible for me at TAH.

I believe the only way you can really enjoy both work and a relaxed life outside of work is to make a clear separation between work and the rest of your life. I believe in separation between work and non-work—not balance. If you are ambitious and driven, you will simply work a *lot*. Jonathan Raymond, an executive coach and the author of *Good Authority,* a management coaching book, makes a really interesting point that I happen to agree with. He says, "The idea of 'work/life balance' has always bugged me...I've always wanted to live in a world where my work and my life were not two things, but one."[80] Talking about work/life balance is creating a false dichotomy, because work is a *part* of life, and has the potential to be a very important and satisfying part of life. I don't think the solution is to diminish the importance of work. Maybe a better phrase would be work/non-work balance.

I know the feeling of being ripped in two as work demands competed with my desire to be home with my family. I wanted to be home, to talk and connect with my wife, throw the ball with my dog, talk to my neighbors in our front yard, and more. At the same time, I wanted to keep solving problems, work with my team, respond to an investor inquiry, prepare a board presentation, or meet with colleagues to make sure the company was moving in the right direction. I wanted to be there with the rest of my company when we needed to finish something time-sensitive.

All this pressure became that much greater with the birth of my daughter in January 2014. Two days after Nora was born, I was back at work, strategizing with my CFO on another round of layoffs that would bring TAH from 100 to 80 employees.

As the weeks and months went on, the guilt I felt if I left work at 6:00 p.m. to have dinner with my wife and do bath time with my daughter before she went to bed was intense, especially since many of my fellow employees were still at the office. Did it matter that I had been working since 6:30 a.m.? Did it matter that right after dinner, I would work at home until 11:00 p.m. or midnight? No, not really. Family time was often invaded by work. Time-sensitive conference calls had to happen. Board members, investment bankers, reporters, and employees did not stop calling, texting, and emailing just because I wanted to be with my family...and even when I was at home I had to step away from my family to talk for hours at a time.

My wife made a book for me on my first Father's Day with pictures of my baby daughter and me doing different things together. One photo caption read, *Nora and Papa like taking walks together. Nora and Papa like eating healthy foods together,* said another. *Another was practicing tummy time together,* and so on. Then there is a photo of my daughter strapped to my chest in a baby carrier while I am talking on my cell phone. That caption says, "Nora and Papa like talking on the phone together." My wife says that she put that page in as a joke, but it makes an important point. I'm sure I was on the phone with my CFO that day, as it was during a time when I talked to him three or four times daily. That page always causes me a little pain. I'm not really present with my daughter; my head is at work. And she isn't enjoying that I'm on my phone—there is no smile on her face. As many parents will tell you, kids really feed off of your energy, and I remember what my energy was like during business phone calls at that time. Six days a week, there was no balance between work and life; it was almost all work. Sometimes I just happened to have a baby strapped to my chest while working.

Each week, I had an oasis from this endless battle for my time—and that was the Sabbath. Every Friday at sunset, I turned off my phone, computer, and iPad, and did not turn them back on until Saturday night. There was no work. There was only life. There were no competing conference calls, emails, or texts. During that interval, my time and focus were primarily for my wife and daughter. And I didn't have to feel guilty about not being at work. Work had already possessed me for the other six days of the week.

I reveled in being Aaron again, not "Work Aaron," not "Aaron, the CEO," not "Aaron, responsible for 125 investors," not "Aaron, responsible for 80 employees and countless vendors." Just Aaron. I could process the week, and I could process my life. I could relax, take walks, and take naps. I could see friends, go out to eat, and enjoy nature. I could have a life.

As CEO, you encounter many challenges, but one of the biggest is working with people. How present are you when you get home if you've just found out that one of your employees suspects another of taking kickbacks? How can you turn work off if you know an employee is dying of brain cancer? How can you be a compassionate husband and father when your company is hemorrhaging cash and you don't know if you'll make payroll? How do you give your company and investors hope when you are downsizing from 180 to 80 employees, and trying to right the ship?

My sincere belief is that if you are driven and ambitious, you may not be able to have what is conventionally seen as a work/life balance, but you must find a way to separate work and non-work, and erect a wall between the two. To put it succinctly: Don't try to balance it; instead, separate it.

A Sale, and Some Hard Questions

By February 2014, we had turned the ship around. TAH had gone from losing over $1 million a month to being at cash-flow break-even. After two successive rounds of layoffs, we had a stable base of 80 employees and a completely new set of C-suite executives, VPs, and operational managers. With only 500 homes previously rented, we were now approaching 2,000 homes rented. We achieved these transformations despite an influx of competing rentals. Six short months after our August restructuring, we were relatively in the clear. However, the turnaround came too late. Investors had become impatient and started pushing for a sale. Instead of producing renewed vigor, for most investors and much of the board, the turnaround only brought relief and the feeling that our moment had passed.

There were fits and starts, but we ultimately sold TAH in April 2015 for $263 million. At the time, that was the largest single sale of homes in U.S. history. The day the sale was announced, I felt a mix of emotions. The American Home had been my life and my baby. What a turn of events from the days of panic and restructuring of 18 months earlier.

I was proud of the turnaround, but couldn't help thinking I had left opportunity on the table. I had had higher hopes for our company and its potential. The company's lifespan had been cut short, and I wondered why. What had I done wrong? How could I have enabled better outcomes so we could have kept growing? In hindsight, I saw that I'd made several mistakes.

I wanted to take the time to reflect on these mistakes, and collect what I learned. There were valuable lessons to be had in terms of operational experience, but there are already numerous books about management turnarounds and operational excellence. After much post-sale reflection, the culprit I zeroed in on was the 24/7 work culture. Now that I am no longer CEO of TAH, I can more clearly see the changes that could have been made within our own company to increase employee satisfaction and productivity, which, in turn, would likely have enhanced our company's performance and increased its longevity. In my opinion, the culture of 24/7 work hurt our company a great deal. I'm writing this book in hopes of changing this culture.

The one day of rest I took each week enabled me personally to operate at a higher level. During those 24 hours, I drew a hard line and took myself completely out of pocket. Could I have pushed more employees to draw this hard line? Would a company policy have helped others disconnect from work and reconnect to their personal lives in a more structured way? Why do so many bright, intelligent, hardworking employees insist on burning themselves out, even when given the opportunity to rest?

Since the sale of The American Home, these are the questions I've taken to heart: is there a way to change our collective mindset around work? How do we stop the workaholic culture? How do we stop taking pride in showing others how many hours we put in? Can we, as business leaders, start to reward good decision-making instead of long hours?

CHAPTER 11

RUB SOME DIRT
IN IT

The price of success is hard work.

—VINCE LOMBARDI

"Rub some dirt in it," coaches used to say after an injury on the field. Players were considered heroic for playing injured, pushing themselves harder than their bodies could handle, and "sucking it up." Shortened careers and life-long injuries were the sacrifices necessary for the sport or team.

As the salaries and value of athletes have skyrocketed, coaches and teams have realized that they can no longer sacrifice their key or star players. The revolution in sports data and sports science has shown the folly of pitching too many pitches in baseball, or a basketball player playing too many minutes. Just think of the cost to a team if LeBron James gets injured. While this is a mercenary view of sports, the financial reward and risk of the continued health of star players is now of paramount concern to coaches and team owners.

"He got his bell rung," was another common refrain. A player staying in the game after a jarring hit to the head was an expected sacrifice. Fans revered players like Junior Seau, who was known for his stoic fortitude and tolerance of pain. Coaches like Bear Bryant were legendary for their grueling practices, long hours, and commitment to winning at all costs.

Unfortunately, "having your bell rung" (read: getting a concussion) is now associated with Lou Gehrig's disease, dementia, and brain damage. Football players are now considered foolish for going back in the game after a head injury, even if the coach coaxes them back into play. And both professional and amateur teams are now taking some measures to prevent head injuries. Why? Because we now know what head injuries do to the brains of football players. We have learned from advances in neuroscience and MRI imaging what really happens when a player receives too many concussions. The brain is a sensitive instrument. (In my opinion, the safety measures are not yet nearly protective enough, given how frightening the results of that brain research are.)

Improve Your Free-Throw Average … While You Sleep

Sports is leading the way toward a more enlightened view of how we think about rest, recovery, and working—or, in this case "playing all the time." Professional sports has moved from valuing toughness at all costs to focusing on peak performance and injury prevention. The investment in players is so high that teams cannot afford to lose any of them to injuries, not to mention the moral obligation owners and teams have to their players. And how do you maintain peak performance while avoiding injury during a long season? By making sure you don't overwork your prime assets: your body and brain.

Most professional and college football teams are systematically limiting practice, especially practice in which tackling is involved. Instead of practicing tackles, top players like the Houston Texans' J. J. Watt now focus on sleeping between eight and eleven hours a night during the season.[81] A 2011 Stanford University study found that encouraging male basketball players to sleep ten hours a day led to an increase in free-throw and three-point shooting success.[82]

Baseball, with its heavy focus on data analytics, has been far ahead of other sports when it comes to understanding the value of rest, recovery, and making sure players do not overwork. Coaches regularly monitor pitch counts, and worry about their best pitchers being in top form. This became a big issue during the 2016 World Series, when Chicago Cubs manager, Joe Maddon, was criticized for overusing his top relief pitcher, Aroldis Chapman, who almost lost game seven. Chapman later critiqued his coach, saying that he had been exhausted.[83]

Hitters can also be affected by hitting too much. A neurology professor at Vanderbilt University, Scott Kutscher, M.D., analyzed every pitch thrown in every Major League game in 2012, and discovered that a hitter's strike zone judgment becomes significantly worse the later it gets in the season.[84] Kutscher theorized that fatigue was a major factor. Most batters are up at the plate every day or every other day, while pitchers have an average of four to five days of rest.

When I started The American Home, I felt as if I was constantly climbing a mountain. Now that strikes me as funny, because when you talk to rock climbers, they tell you that rest is the key to becoming a better climber. Train hard, rest, repeat.

The argument in rock climbing circles isn't whether to take a break, but how long the break should be. After an intense climb, do you take one day or three days? Renowned competitive rock climber and X Games champion Katie Brown recounts the frustration she used to feel when she would have to take three days off from climbing to travel between competitions. But she now believes those days of enforced rest saved her from serious injury. "Your body is temporarily weakened after a period of rigorous training. It reacts to this weakened state by rebuilding itself to better execute its designated task the next time. Although often overlooked, rest is quite possibly the most important aspect of any training program," says Brown.[85]

By taking a break, Brown argues, rock climbers enable themselves to climb harder and farther. The business world could learn a great deal from climbers like Katie Brown.

Golf, like rock climbing, is a mentally challenging sport in which success or failure rests on the actions of a single individual. Rory McIlroy is one of the top golfers in the world. In 2007, when he was 18 years old and playing in his first Open tournament, he was asked to describe himself. He said, "I like to go out and go to the cinema, try and think about golf as little as possible when I'm off the golf course, and just try to lead a normal life."[86] In 2011, after he won his first major, that changed. "As a 22-year-old, it's very easy to be taken by it—meeting all these people and thinking it's cool: 'Oh, I've got such-and-such's number!' 'I just hung out with whoever last night!' You're enjoying yourself and having a great time, but it's not…fulfilling." He described feeling homesick during tournaments, and his game suffered. He came to realize how important down time with friends and family was. For McIlroy, top performance requires that separation between golfing and celebrity on the one hand, and normal life on the other.

Elite basketball players have described needing to use that off switch, too. LeBron James and Stephen Curry, considered the best two players in the NBA, both make a choice to turn off social media during the playoffs to focus on their game when it matters most. Leading up to the 2015 NBA playoffs, James said, "I don't have no phones, no social media, I don't have anything .... I don't care about nonsense. There's too much nonsense out there. Not during this time, this is when I lock in right now and I don't need nothing creeping into my mind that don't need to be there." James calls his social media blackout "Zero Dark Thirty-23." (The "23" is his jersey number.)[87]

If You're Going to be Miserable, You Might as Well Get Some Exercise

Many elite athletes come to train with Dr. Marcus Elliott at his sports training centers in Santa Barbara, California. Operating on the cutting edge of sports medicine and training, Elliott uses computers and sensors to break down the physical mechanics of an athlete's stride, jump, side step, and other movements. This allows his team to determine exactly where an athlete's greatest risk of injury lies. Athletes learn that a small tweak to the way they have been shooting a basketball or throwing a pitch can lead to a longer and more successful career.

Elliott knows that helping athletes perform better physically is only half the battle. He works to prepare them mentally, as well. Through techniques that help athletes discover the furthest limits of their physical and mental abilities, Elliott's training affects their minds as well as their bodies. An example of this is Elliot's take on the Japanese water purification ritual *misogi.* In Elliot's version, the trainee tries to find the limits to what they think they can do, and then push through those limits. Elliot works with the trainee on creating a challenge they think is 50 percent possible, then he does due diligence to make sure the challenge will not harm the athlete; and then he joins the athlete in the challenge.

Elliot's *misogi* exercise with NBA player Kyle Korver consisted of paddle-boarding 30 miles from the Channel Islands to Santa Barbara (a boat with medical staff was following their journey). Elliot paddled right along with Korver. Korver had had limited experience on a paddle board, and he told me he decided ahead of time that the only way he would be able to make the trip was by having the most efficient possible stroke. So, before the challenge began, he spent some time breaking down his stroke in order to perfect it. When he collapsed on shore after the grueling challenge, he asked himself why he had never mentally broken down the way he shoots a basketball in the same way. So that was what he set about doing. The very next season, he broke the NBA three-point record. The *misogi* exercise was meant not to prove how tough Korver was, but to provide a mental breakthrough to improve his own performance.

So, what does *misogi* have to do with taking a break? Did Korver shoot more basketballs to break the three-point record? No, he didn't. Was he using his phone obsessively while paddling? Of course not. Was he thinking about basketball during his *misogi* exercise? No; all he could do was focus on the task at hand.

The Sabbath isn't just resting or sleeping all day. As we will discuss later, a hard break is about doing something different that will allow you to rest your brain and to potentially achieve some higher insight or understanding. In their own way, Korver and Elliott were taking a Sabbath out in the middle of the ocean.

The ocean is actually a great place for a Sabbath, because it is really hard to be texting or calling. I think this is one reason so many Silicon Valley and tech entrepreneurs love to surf. Surfing is their Sabbath, their hard break. Surfing can be very demanding, but talk to surfers, and they will talk about the peace of mind and refreshmentit can bring.

Misogi is only one of the tools Elliott uses in his practice. Another is rest. Elliott told me that when he was a student at Harvard Medical School, he decided to devote 100 percent of his waking hours to studying. So he stopped exercising. Soon after, his academic performance began to suffer. So he started drinking coffee to stay awake longer and study even harder. He then slept terribly, and struggled even more in school.

Miserable, Elliott finally told himself that if he was going to fail, he might as well go back to what he loved, and started to exercise again. He dialed studying back to 60 percent of his waking hours, cut way back on coffee, and focused on sleep and exercise. It wasn't long before he rocketed to the top of his class.

This has been an enduring lesson for him. Elliott has numerous high-profile clients, and has opened a new state-of-the-art facility in partnership with Emory University and the Atlanta Hawks, and yet he still takes five weeks of vacation every summer, during which he maintains limited phone and email access. It is his time to spend with family. He comes back rejuvenated, with new insights and ideas, excited at the prospect of re-engaging with his work. His hard break enables him to do more, work harder, and sustain success over the long term.

And you see this over and over again in sports now. Work hard, rest hard. Creating hard breaks and resets is the key to long-term performance and long-term health and success in sports. Most non-sports careers last far longer, and, in that way, are more demanding than sports careers. We wear our sports heroes' jerseys, hang on their every word, and try to emulate the best coaches, so why not follow the sports world's lead? Why not place limits, and take hard breaks to protect ourselves, and maintain performance over the long haul?

CHAPTER 12

A CEO WHO PAYS EMPLOYEES TO GO ON VACATION, AND OTHER BIZARRE TALES

*If you go dark on vacation, you will be
ready for the light when you return.*
—BRIAN SCUDAMORE, CEO OF O2E BRANDS

Think Days and Free Days

More than a decade ago, Brian Scudamore's life was falling apart. He was working himself to exhaustion on his first company, 1-800-GOT-JUNK?, but it wasn't growing. His marriage had ended, and he and his ex-wife were splitting the demands of co-parenting a newborn. He was headed for complete burnout, both professionally and personally. Then, on a walk in a forest near his house, Brian had the epiphany that he needed to re-prioritize his life. "I realized that the 7-to-7 grind was obscuring breakthrough ideas and making difficult decisions even harder," he said.

Scudamore decided to add two counterintuitive days into his week. Mondays became what he calls Think Days, and Fridays became known as Free Days. "On Think Days, I don't go into the office or take meetings. Instead, I structure my day around identifying my biggest priorities for the week and month ahead...Still, it's the Friday Free Day that is probably most counterintuitive—and the most important. I've taken Fridays off for the past five years. They're days where I do what I love—skiing with my children, cooking, learning languages, and biking."

"When I'm away from the office, things have time to marinate. Connections bubble up and often turn into big, business-changing ideas," Scudamore says. For example, he and his team had been struggling for a year to create a great logo and look for his second company. Then, one Friday as he was treating himself to gelato, he saw a smiley face made of lemon peels in the gelato store, and all of a sudden thought of the image that became his company's logo. "Free Day gave me a vision I never would have had sitting in the office."

"The future of knowledge work isn't about people sitting in front of computers and meeting-room tables. It's not competing to work the longest hours and still feeling behind. Instead, the future of knowledge work is leaders leading lifestyles that help them feel positive, relaxed, and creative so that they can set better priorities, set better examples for their people, and have more breakthrough ideas," Scudamore says.

This belief system also includes the six-week vacation Scudamore takes every year: "I realized that unless I completely unplug on vacation, I cheat myself out of generating fresh, creative ideas. In the long run, business suffers from my burnout." He is so serious about unplugging for six weeks that he has his assistant change the passwords on his email and social media accounts. He has been doing this for eight years, and comes back from vacation feeling super-charged.

John Roa is another CEO who believes in vacations and time off. A serial entrepreneur, Roa founded a digital engagement consultancy that was one of the fastest-growing companies in the country. In 2014, he sold that company to Salesforce.com, and has since started the venture capital firm Roa Ventures, as well as a nonprofit called Digital Hope.

Roa finds that international travel refreshes his mind and opens up new vistas of thinking. "There's a tremendous opportunity when traveling to allow yourself to think in ways that you normally don't," he says.

He describes his working life as being "like a glass that fills up slowly with perpetually dripping water—daily stresses, decisions, and the pressures of work." When the glass starts to fill, my thinking becomes clouded, and productivity declines." Traveling, for him, is like dumping out the glass.[88]

Maybe CEOs like Scudamore and Roa are just coming around to a very old idea. John Pierpont Morgan, a man who dominated finance and banking in the late 19th and early 20th centuries, and whose name graces the banking behemoth J. P. Morgan, was obsessed with rest. He claimed that he "could do a year's work in nine months—but not in twelve months." In other words, he took a three-month vacation every year![89]

That's all fine and good for the CEO. The question is: could every employee in the company take a hard break without the organization falling apart?

The answer is yes. Scudamore has rolled out a policy of making sure all employees to go dark while on vacation.[90] This required some coordination and planning in advance, but he is convinced that it improves profits, productivity, and engagement. An added benefit has been learning where the pain points are in his company's organizational chart. If a person cannot leave for vacation and delegate their job to another person or team without significant problems, something is wrong. To Scudamore and his company, that is a big red flag. He even has employees make sure their vacationing teammates are not checking in.[91]

How to Earn $7,500—by Not Working

Scudamore is not alone. A new generation of entrepreneurs is realizing that working on vacation doesn't make sense. Bart Lorang, CEO and co-founder of the contact management platform FullContact, pays his employees $7,500 to unplug from technology while on vacation. Lorang calls his policy "Paid, Paid Vacation."

"It's really important to unplug to become a human again," he said, especially for those like programmers who work with technology.[92] For Lorang, Paid, Paid Vacation is a perk to help recruit employees and boost morale. It seems to be working, as the company has been voted one of the Best Places to Work by *Outside* magazine for three years running, in addition to winning awards for its software products.[93]

Science backs up these initiatives. A fascinating 2012 study from the University of California at Santa Barbara shows that when people pause from mentally challenging tasks and give their minds a rest while they do something undemanding (using a smartphone does not count!), this substantially improves their performance of the mentally challenging task. What's interesting about this study is that it shows that doing something mentally undemanding is ultimately better for the subjects' performance than completely resting.[94] It's an important point that taking a Sabbath doesn't mean not doing anything or sleeping all day, but actually doing things that refresh and rest your mind. When we go on vacation, we still do things like swim in the ocean, hike a mountain, or cook and enjoy family and friends. It turns out these things are not only enjoyable in themselves, but they also help us rise to the challenges of work when we return.

Another study, from financial giant Intuit, reports that 82 percent of small business owners experienced an increase in job performance after a vacation.[95] Again, it's not really surprising that when people return from vacation, they are refreshed and probably excited to come back to the challenges of work. I always find that on Saturday night or Sunday morning, when I re-engage with work, I'm excited to see what I have missed, and to work on tough problems—or even edit a book I've been working on for three years (yes, I'm talking about this book!).

The problem with vacations is that we generally take them only a few times a year—and most of us go for a shorter stint than the three months J. P. Morgan took. Studies have shown that the benefits of vacations—lower stress, higher cognitive abilities, and higher levels of happiness—dissipate within two to four weeks.[96]

This is why Brian Scudamore takes his weekly Free Days and Think Days. His company 1-800-GOT-JUNK? was struggling to grow a dozen years ago, but has since become part of a group of brands owned by Scudamore that produced upward of $250 million in revenue in 2016, and now employs more than 400 people. He has gone on to create other successful startups, has appeared on TV shows such as *Undercover Boss,* and has been profiled in publications such as *The Wall Street Journal.* Taking one full day off and spending another day just thinking catapulted Scudamore to a successful business life and a more enjoyable personal life.

Scudamore says, "My father was one of the top surgeons in Canada, so when I was young, I saw how surgeons aim to have maximum impact with minimum intervention... Accomplishing this is about careful planning. The actual surgery—the physical work—is only a small part of the process. I approach business the same way. The Mondays I devote to thinking allow me to operate with surgical precision during the rest of the week."[97]

Enlightened, high-functioning, driven CEOs and entrepreneurs recharge, re-energize, and sustain their success by taking clear, unequivocal breaks from work. Some of them have taken it a step further, and recognized that what benefits them will also benefit their employees and their companies, as well. Built-in hard breaks are a necessary ingredient for long-term success, not only for individuals, but also for entire organizations.

CHAPTER 13

LIFT YOUR LEGS
OUT OF THE MUD

Most people overestimate what they can do in one year,
and underestimate what they can do in ten years.

—BILL GATES

The Marathon

Life, and especially work life, is filled with adversity, challenges, failures, and unexpected twists and turns. Being able to roll with these is the key to having a successful life and career. I've told you two stories about how I responded to setbacks in my work life. The first took place in 2003, when my response to my underperforming fund was to stand in the shower and cry. The second was in 2012–2013, when The American Home had a major cash-flow problem and I was in danger of not making payroll; this time, I remained resolute and strong, and took the hard steps to fix the problem. What was the difference between me in 2003 and me in 2013? In 2003, I was fragile. In 2013, I was resilient. That resilience—that strong foundation and balance—flowed from my observance of the Sabbath.

David Wolpe, the Rabbi of Temple Sinai in Los Angeles, says, "The secret of success is stamina. It is wonderful to have gifts, but I have known extravagantly gifted people who cannot lift their legs out of the mud."[98]

Life moves by in a flash and a blur. By stepping off life's bullet train and resting, I have allowed myself critical time to recover mentally, physically, and psychologically. This recovery time has become crucial to my resilience, which is the key to long-term success. People underestimate the importance of the long term. People who overwork without regular periods of recovery are like someone who's attempting to run a marathon by sprinting the whole way. At some point they're going to find themselves lying at the edge of the road clutching their side.

We already know from the research and studies presented earlier in this book that overwork makes you fragile. Remember the medical interns who are more likely to be in a car accident after an extended shift? Remember John Pencavel's study showing how efficiency decreases as overtime increases? And then there are the harrowing space shuttle stories demonstrating that overwork makes people more prone to make mistakes. And the Harvard-Stanford study showing that stress at work leads to poor health. An increased likelihood of getting sick or dying is the very definition of being fragile.

"We live in a world that celebrates work and activity, ignores renewal and recovery, and fails to recognize that both are necessary for sustained performance," argue Tony Schwartz and Dr. Jim Loehr in their book, *The Power of Full Engagement*. Loehr is CEO of the Human Performance Institute. For 30 years, he has trained executives and athletes to achieve high performance and full engagement in high-stress environments. Tony Schwartz is the president and founder of The Energy Project, a consultancy that helps organizations to be more engaged and sustain higher performance. Their book's central argument is that energy management—and not time spent working—is the key to high performance.[99] They maintain that squeezing more and more work into a day is not the key to success. If we are working 24/7, never disconnecting and racing around with nonstop busy schedules, we are not even trying to manage our energy. And yet doing so is what will help us achieve our best performance in the marathon of life.

Loehr and Schwartz are puzzled at the way most people and organizations view recovery and taking a break. "Sadly, the need for recovery is often viewed as evidence of weakness rather than as an integral aspect of sustained performance."

After studying and working with thousands of individuals, including star athletes and top executives, they found that "the richest, happiest, and most productive lives are characterized by an ability to fully engage in the challenge at hand, but also an ability to disengage periodically and seek renewal."[100]

The World Does Not Need Your Assistance to Turn

Another thing that makes you more resilient is realizing that you aren't as important as you think you are—in your work life, that is. This was a humbling experience for me. When I started taking a Sabbath, I realized that the world didn't stop if I stopped responding to emails and texts, or stopped checking what was happening in the world markets. Business deals and news events happen with or without me. The world keeps turning. It doesn't need my assistance to do so.

That powerful experience reminded me of who I was and who I was not. I was not this all-powerful CEO, nor was I the person who kept the company afloat all by himself. I was someone who needed a break to just simply be Aaron. It gave me some much-needed perspective. It also taught me that it's okay to shed my fantasy of complete sacrifice for the company and its investors—and my fantasy that I carried the weight of the world on my shoulders—one day a week. This perspective keeps me grounded and helps me make decisions that are not based on emotion or ego. This has proven extremely helpful.

Here's a concrete example: when I was CEO of The American Home, there came a moment when my board of directors recommended I take a 70 percent cut to my salary. This came right after they'd given me some brutal feedback about my job performance, given the operational problems of the company. Some of the feedback was deserved and some was not, in my opinion. What was not in question, however, was the performance of the company. My younger self would have taken this insult to my ego and either self-flagellated or raged at my board—or both. Instead, I removed my ego from the equation and asked which response from me would be best for the company, and which response would align with my most important values. My company was in trouble, and regardless of what my ego was trying to tell me, I needed to do my best to right the ship. So, I didn't self-flagellate, and I didn't give the board a piece of my mind. I took the pay cut they recommended and took the necessary steps to fix the company. Going through this process has made me personally more resilient. Without reflection, and time to process and put aside my ego, I would not have lasted as CEO. And I certainly wouldn't have been able to lead the company not only through a restructuring, but also to a successful sale.

Randy Gold, who was president of a large accounting firm for many years, told me something that resonated with my own experience. He said that when he celebrated the Sabbath, it reminded him that "I am not the most important, central person on earth." For Senator Joseph Lieberman, the Sabbath liberated him from the pressure and ego of Washington politics, reminded him of what was truly important, and helped him sustain a long and successful career.

The mythologist, writer, and lecturer Joseph Campbell said, "Opportunities to find deeper powers within ourselves come when life seems most challenging."[101] That is exactly what happened to Matt Auron several years ago, when he was the Director of Wisdom at the health care giant Davita, a company that specializes in kidney care and dialysis. Auron was responsible for global culture and leadership in an enterprise with 65,000 employees and annual revenues of $15 billion.

The problem was that Auron was spiraling downward due to overwork and the effects of a grueling schedule. He was smoking and drinking, and at age 32, he went to the hospital with what he thought was a heart attack. Soon he was taking Xanax, and he reached the breaking point while on a flight to India. Auron experienced a powerful panic attack that felt like a heart attack on the plane. "My operating system was breaking down," he said. "The relentless fast pace was toxic to my body." How ironic is it that his title was Director of Wisdom?

Auron left the company to work on regaining his health. He vowed not to work at night, and to force himself to take one day off a week. "When you are a young man, you can push your body, but as you get older, you can't," he said. Auron experienced a deeper shift that forced him to confront his ego, shame, family history, and the deep dark self that he calls "the dragon." In my conversation with Auron, he said it was only when he confronted his darker self that he started operating from a stronger foundation, which allowed him to grow and mature.

Auron decided to create a firm called Evolution Consulting, which offers executive coaching to CEOs and other business leaders in order to allow them to take advantage of what he learned the hard way. He forces executives to answer important questions such as, "Who do I really want to be?" He wants them to go on a deep journey to their sacred space, where they can find themselves again and again. Auron says that when you go deep and a transition happens, "you awaken into a different maturity and a new way of being. You are reborn."

Executives everywhere are struggling with nonstop activity, and are reaching out for help. Executive coaching is now estimated to be a $1-billion-a-year business. Companies are taking it so seriously that some are rolling out big, expensive programs. Johnson & Johnson has launched a $100,000-per-executive-per-year program to prevent burnout for seven of its key people.[102] The program includes therapists, coaches, and physical exercise.

Auron says executives come to him because "they are in pain or are struggling. They want to exhibit a higher quality of leadership, or they are battling for capacity in their life." According to Auron, most CEOs are trying to "level up," or take their leadership abilities to the next level. This generally means giving up responsibility and not micromanaging. When executives can't bear to give up the steering wheel and experience the symptoms of burnout, they ask for help.

An executive coach is a type of support system for a driven, high-powered person. How does Auron help executives succeed in all facets of their lives while enduring all the pressures that come with being a CEO? He has found that you need to pull back, take hard breaks, and give yourself the time to go deep and work on yourself in order to become a better leader and a better person. Auron is more than just a coach; he is also an independent resource, therapist, sounding board, and advisor.

Auron says, "I still work hard and feel stress, but there is a qualitative difference." He is now on a sustainable path. And his new firm is flourishing—apparently, there are a lot of stressed-out, overworked executives looking for help. Despite the hard work of growing a firm, he said, "I could never go back to my old habits." By taking the hard break and re-evaluating his life, Auron emerged as a changed man, and is currently helping other executives change their lives, as well.

The Overkill Cult

And what is true for top-level executives is true for everyone else, as well.

It is many people's dream to quit their office job, work remotely, set their own schedule, and travel around the world. These days, Jason Lengstorf is doing just that. And contrary to what you might expect, Jason is neither wealthy nor a CEO.

In 2012, Lengstorf was working 70 to 90 hours a week at a technology company. He had lost touch with many of his friends, was not exercising, and weighed more than at any other time in his life. On top of all that, he had just landed the biggest project of his career: creating a Black Friday sales site for a Fortune 100 company. To meet the client's goal and deliver before Black Friday, he skipped Thanksgiving, and slept only six hours in four days.

The client was pleased when Lengstorf delivered a wonderful finished product. But his reward was total exhaustion, burnout, and the weird side effect of having his beard turn white and fall out. He was miserable and wiped out, and finally realized enough was enough.[103]

Lengstorf's story sounds eerily like the one of a promising young accountant we hired at The American Home. This guy was a rock star. No matter what we threw at him, he knocked it out of the park. We gave him more responsibility and promoted him. When we started staff cutbacks, our CFO felt that this young accountant could handle more and more duties. In hindsight, if I had paid closer attention, I would have realized something was wrong. He started taking more and more sick days as regular head colds and stomach bugs kept him out of the office. Then, one day, he didn't call or come in. When we finally got hold of him, he told us he wasn't coming back. He was completely burned out. I felt terribly responsible. This came at a time when we were running a really lean and mean operation. His absence hurt, and it was our fault.

After Lengstorf realized how painful overwork and a heavy schedule had become, he quit, sold everything, and began to travel the world. As part of his new approach to life, Lengstorf has cut his hours in half, and now works remotely. He travels extensively, and has written articles and blog posts so others can follow his example.

To his shock, Lengstorf finds that he is more productive than he has ever been. His turnaround times on projects have gone down, and he consistently hits deadlines. He says:

> I know that taking breaks makes me more productive. Time away from work lets my passion and excitement for the work renew itself. Taking my mind off a project allows my subconscious to roll around abstract ideas that result in better solutions. Breaks from the job lower my stress levels and boost my creativity. So, I make sure to take time off, even if my gut (incorrectly) tells me it's a bad idea.

> I take walks. I leave my phone in my pocket when I'm out with friends or eating my meals. I spend a fair amount of time on hobbies like writing and hunting for the world's best cheeseburger. I'm happier today than I can ever remember being. I feel excited to work on my projects, to pursue my hobbies, and to spend time with the people I love. I'm excited to be alive.

Lengstorf is adamant that working long hours has nothing to do with productivity. Instead, he says, "The overkill cult is a cultural delusion that working 60 hours a week is somehow honorable." I love how he calls it a cult, because cults are more interested in controlling group behavior than obtaining actual outcomes. Cults normally come with serious downsides, and this one is no different.

CHAPTER 14

THIS IS YOUR
BRAIN ON
DOWNTIME

Idleness is not just a vacation, an indulgence or a vice;
it is as indispensable to the brain as vitamin D is to the body.
—TIM KREIDER, "THE 'BUSY' TRAP"

Consider that your brain consumes 20 percent of all the energy your body produces, but makes up only two percent of your body weight. This power-hungry organ is a beast.[104]

Just how powerful is the brain? Science has shown that thinking can make you physically weaker. Scientist J.C. Welch measured the physical strength of people who were squeezing a lever. When they performed a mental task at the same time, the physical force they exerted was reduced by as much as 50 percent.[105]

Clearing Toxins from Our Brains

Even with all our advanced technology, it is difficult for science to understand what is going on with our 86 billion neurons and their 100 trillion connections. And we are just starting to uncover some of the brain's secrets, such as how and when it clears away toxins. Research has shown that when the brain is awake, and most busy, it puts off clearing away waste that has accumulated in the spaces between brain cells. This is especially worrisome, because the long-term buildup of certain toxins and chemicals seems to have a link to Alzheimer's. The brain restores itself when we are less mentally active or asleep.[106]

Most of us are not thinking about clearing toxins from our brains. We are too busy trying to clear our inbox. A 2010 LexisNexis survey of 1,700 white collar workers in five countries, including the U.S., found that participants spent more than half their average workday simply managing information. Half of these said the deluge of data had them at the breaking point. It would be safe to guess that this has only become worse since the study came out.

Managing a torrent of information is hard, especially since (despite what we may believe and how we behave) our brains are not computers. Robert Epstein, senior research psychologist at The American Institute for Behavioral Research & Technology in California, explains that the computer metaphor for the brain is a faulty historical one that needs to be retired:

> Computers quite literally *process information*... We don't store words or the rules that tell us how to manipulate them. We don't create representations of visual stimuli, store them in a short-term memory buffer, and then transfer the representation into a long-term memory device. We don't retrieve information or images or

words from memory registers. Computers do all of these things, but organisms do not.[107]

Computers don't daydream, but people do. When we are daydreaming or relaxing, the brain doesn't slow down. In fact, quite the opposite happens. Recent research tells us that downtime "replenishes the brain's stores of attention and motivation, encourages productivity and creativity, and is essential to both achieve our highest levels of performance and simply form stable memories in everyday life."[108]

There is an area of the brain that neurologists call the default mode network, which uses downtime from activity to try to make sense of what the brain has recently learned. This part of the brain considers problems, patterns, and memories—all while we think we are not doing anything. Creative people in particular have a more active default mode network than others.

Several studies have shown that simple daydreaming helps you solve tough problems, form new memories, learn new languages, and improve overall performance. MRI scans have shown that the brain, and specifically the default mode network, is extremely active when individuals are resting.

Psychologist Tony Crabbe reports that a research group at Carnegie Mellon found that people are the limiting factor for computers today. Specifically, it is "our lack of ability to focus and think."[109] The study found that with computers and the internet speeding up, people have trouble keeping up with the speed of information and dealing with distractions. While computers are becoming capable of doing more and more tasks, people are not. "In doing more and more, we are thinking less and less," Crabbe explains. "In an information age, it is our cognitive abilities that matter."

Giving our brains a break and allowing time for reflection improves our performance. A study done in Bangalore, India, at one of the largest Indian information-technology service companies, explored what happened when employees were given time in the work day to reflect on what they were doing. Employees who were given that time to reflect outperformed those who were not by up to 25 percent. And these results were achieved with just 15 minutes of reflection time.[110] Imagine if the employees had been given a whole day. When we take the time for reflection, we are increasing our chances of making better decisions and avoiding making bad ones. Good decisions take energy. If you're working all the time, how can you be sure that you are making the right decisions?

"There is nothing quite so useless as doing with great efficiency something that should not be done at all," said the management guru Peter Drucker. What if a lot of the work we are doing is counterproductive? If we don't spend enough time reflecting, and instead manically jump from one busy activity to another, we could be counterproductive without realizing it. I can think of many times that I have been guilty of this. As an investor, one of the worst mistakes you can make is to constantly turn over your portfolio of investments. Between increased transaction costs and increased taxes, your long-term performance can suffer. Jumping from one stock to another or not letting a winning stock continue its run-up can really hurt your performance. It's really hard to not do very much, especially when so many different stocks are winning and losing every day. But the best investors, such as Warren Buffett, actually aren't very active; they are downright lethargic. In this world that values constant motion, it can be difficult to sit still, but investing is one endeavor where the value of sitting still is abundantly evident.

PayPal co-founder and venture capitalist Peter Thiel found his first success after realizing he and his company were not using their time in a productive way. In his bestselling book, *Zero to One,* he recounts how his company Confinity was deadlocked in a heated competition to be the top online payment-processing company with rival X.com, Elon Musk's firm at the time. Everyone was putting in 100-hour workweeks and getting nowhere. Finally, instead of continuing a losing battle, Thiel took a big step back and realized that it would be much smarter to merge together. PayPal was born, and the fierce competition was over.[III] Not to mention the fact that by combining forces with the likes of Elon Musk, Thiel's company acquired a huge storehouse of talent.

Solutions to seemingly intractable problems are often available if you're not too burned out to come up with them. Are you giving yourself enough time to recover, reflect, and make good decisions? For one day a week, you could step outside your normal working habits and get a little distance and perspective.

I actually wish I had reflected more on the state of The American Home when we were growing too fast. If we had slowed down in late 2012, the company would have experienced less pain and made more money, had I reflected on the capabilities of the company and not been so determined to grow as fast as possible to beat the competition. Maybe this is why Brad Feld, in addition to his digital Sabbath, takes an additional week every quarter, and why Brian Scudamore has a think day.

Leonardo da Vinci and Kanye West
Leonardo da Vinci once said, "The greatest geniuses accomplish more when they work less." Back in the 15th century, he got in trouble for this philosophy.

Leonardo's patron had become frustrated with the progress of his latest work, the famous painting of the Last Supper. Leonardo pushed back and wrote to his sponsor, "It is a very good plan every now and then to go away and have a little relaxation. When you come back to the work your judgment will be surer, since to remain constantly at work will cause you to lose the power of judgment."[112]

Where do your new ideas and insights come to you? If you answered "in the shower," you have that in common with 72 percent of the population, according to a study from the University of Pennsylvania. Why? Our brains are establishing new connections and patterns unconsciously, and the brain, given the space and time, revels in relaxation. The more relaxed we are, the more open we are to innovative and creative insights.[113]

When do most people experience free time and relaxation? On vacation. That's exactly how the idea for the smash Broadway hit *Hamilton* came to its creator, Lin-Manuel Miranda. The concept for one of the most inventive Broadway shows in decades didn't come together in an office. He picked up Ron Chernow's biography of Alexander Hamilton as a vacation read and got sucked into the story. The lesson, according to Miranda, is: "You can have good ideas when you take a break from what you are normally doing and not going 100 miles an hour."[114]

He is not alone. The rapper Kanye West, who has won 21 Grammy awards, announced in 2016 that he was getting rid of his phone so he "could have air to create."[115] Kanye is known for his ego and eccentricity, but he is deadly serious about creativity. In a speech to students at Oxford University, he also said, "I can literally hear a whisper and it'll, like, throw off my stream of consciousness." When he needs to create, he doesn't want distractions. He doesn't want busyness.[116]

Artists from Leonardo to Kanye have thrived on down time, but they are not the only creative people who benefit from taking time away from being busy. Nobel Prize-winning physicist Steven Weinberg was nagged by the problem of how nuclear reactions produce the heat of the sun, until the answer just came to him one day as he was driving around Boston in his red Chevy Camaro.[117]

Albert Einstein was famous for taking breaks. He said, "I take time to go for long walks on the beach so that I can listen to what is going on inside my head. If my work isn't going well, I lie down in the middle of a workday and gaze at the ceiling while I listen and visualize what goes on in my imagination." Einstein was also famous for taking a mile-and-a-half walk every day with no socks on.[118]

As we have shown, the same holds true for creative people in the business world. When Bill Gates was CEO of Microsoft, he would regularly go to a secluded location for what he called a "Think Week," to get away from the demands and distractions of work.[119] Gates would have to take a helicopter or small seaplane to get to a small waterfront home secluded in the Pacific Northwest. There, all visitors were barred except for a caretaker who would slip him two simple meals a day.[120]

In a world where information is now a commodity, innovation becomes very valuable. Not to put too fine a point on it, we cannot innovate without our brains. And it has become increasingly clear that we impede innovation when we do not give our brains an opportunity to rest. It is also clear that

Americans have fallen out of the habit of simply taking time to daydream and think. Shockingly, a recent survey by the Bureau of Labor Statistics found that 83 percent of Americans say they spend no time "relaxing or thinking."[121] Paying attention to creative leaders in the arts, the sciences, and business is very instructive in this regard. To put it another way: anytime I can place myself in the company of Albert Einstein, Leonardo da Vinci, and Bill Gates, sign me up.

CHAPTER 15

LONELINESS IS DANGEROUS

There's simply no real substitute for physical presence.
—FRANK BRUNI, "THE MYTH OF QUALITY TIME"

The genius of the Sabbath is that it is one day when the rush of time slows. Busy schedules and constant emailing and texting stop. So, what do you have time for when everything else disappears? Your family is one of the biggest beneficiaries.

"I only see the top of your head now," my wife used to say when I was running The American Home and constantly checking my phone for the latest email or communication from one of my employees. During one argument, my wife became so upset with my unhealthy relationship with my phone that she threw it in the bushes. On Shabbat, my phone is off, and I have ample time to spend with my wife and children.

The difficulty of balancing work and personal life is largely due to the fact that, because of smartphones and the internet, the boundaries between the two are much harder to maintain. Add in the hundreds if not thousands of people we are connected to on social media. What gets crowded out is family. We are distracted even as our spouses and children desperately try to get our attention.

The changing demographics of the workforce have also put increased stress on families. In 1960, only 40 percent of children lived in households where both parents worked at least part-time outside the home. Now, it is 60 percent. According to a recent Pew survey, working parents say that balancing work and family is difficult, and that "parenting is tiring and stressful."[122]

The Sabbath offers a solution. One day a week, it's all family and no work. There's no balancing simply a hard break from work. You know at least once a week, your family is getting all of you, not some stressed-out person who is being pulled in every direction.

Lessons from the Accidental Sabbath

Film producer Thomas Barad started taking a Sabbath later in life, when he was in his fifties. One of his favorite family memories comes from a day that wasn't the Sabbath, but became a Sabbath-like experience. It was summer in Los Angeles in the mid-1990s, and the temperature had climbed to 110 degrees. On a Thursday night, the power went out in wide swaths of the city, including the Barad household. This was before cell phones, so things really ground to a halt. With no power, the whole family–two teenage boys and Barad and his wife–gathered in the kitchen and started playing games. Games led to conversations and laughter. Disconnected from TV, computers, and other distractions, they connected with each other, instead.

Two or three hours flew by, as the family had nothing else to do but to enjoy one another's company.

Suddenly, there was a whir, and the power came back on. TVs came to life all over the house, and soon, everyone, especially the children, rushed back to their rooms. All you could hear was doors slamming as the members of the family retreated to their own private worlds. The next day, at the family's regular Friday-night Shabbat dinner, Barad told them they had experienced the Sabbath the previous day. This is what the Sabbath is supposed to be: time with each other, with few distractions and filled with connection.

Despite the allure of technology and instant entertainment, children really do want their parents around. Studies show that simply being physically close to your children will have certain benefits, including the improved psychological health that can make adolescents and teenagers less likely to have drug and alcohol problems.[123, 124]

However, for some people, the sad reality is that work may be less stressful than home life. For them, work is an escape, and home life is the source of stress. Some are in frustrating marriages or struggle to handle a busy family schedule. The idea of a day with no distractions from family life might seem like torture. What happens if home life is hard, and work is an escape?

Ignoring problems doesn't make them go away or help them get better. It generally does quite the opposite. The uncomfortable truth is that when you stop focusing on work, you might have to come face to face with the larger issues you've been avoiding. Emailing and texting your way past difficulties is not the way to a happy and sustainable life.

Another problem may arise when family schedules become as busy as a day at the office. When your non-work activities–from shopping to soccer, ballet practice, piano lessons, and so on–become as stressful to manage as your work life, it may be time for a re-think. If not just you, but your whole family takes a break at least one day a week, you all may be happier. Soccer and ballet are great, but you may actually be making it harder to connect to your family if all of you spend the weekend racing from one activity to the next to the next. All the racing creates stress, and it's hard to have strong ties to your family if you are stressed out while you're around them. Just as the brain needs down time to create neural connections, so you and your loved ones need down time to create interpersonal connections.

The Health Benefits of Face-to-Face Connection

According to a 2002 study by the University of Illinois, the most common factor in the 10 percent of people who experienced the highest levels of happiness and the fewest signs of depression were their ties to friends and family, and the commitment they had to spending time with them. One of the researchers said, "Word needs to be spread. It is important to work on social skills, close interpersonal ties, and social support in order to be happy."[125]

I recently met a man with a powerful story that corroborates this research. His name is Norman Thoms, a cyber-security specialist with the insurance company Munich Re. He told me about one particular Christmas, when his son was three years old:

> I was looking around the living room at all the new toys scattered around. As I sat on the couch, my son came walking into the living room and looked at all the toys, too. He stood there for a moment,

and then walked over and sat next to me on the couch. He simply wanted to be next to me. That was really when it hit me. He just wanted to sit with Dad. There isn't a toy in the world that could satisfy a child's desire to feel loved and comforted by his parents. I began thinking that it wasn't the toys that made my kids happy, it was the time they spend with us.

It began to dawn on him that when it came to holidays, the toys were secondary, and the togetherness was primary. He remembers talking to his mother about it, saying she didn't have to bring a present for the kids when she came over– "they just want to spend time with you. I've always had a close-knit Italian family, and we've always spent time together during the holidays, birthdays, and anniversaries... so this wasn't anything new. But the idea of not buying toys, and simply spending focused time together was a bit of a change. I'm not saying that there were no more toys purchased for our kids... it just began a slow process of limiting the toys and focusing more on the time spent together." Thoms calls it "trading toys for time," and it has had a subtle but profound effect on his family.

Not only family bonds, but friendships, too, are strengthened by the Sabbath. The Sabbath grants you time to be with the friends you find yourself wishing you had the time for.

It is as important to maintain close friendships as to have strong bonds with your family. Friends can bring us a lifetime of happiness, satisfaction, and joy. If you are constantly busy with work and a hectic schedule, friends are an easy thing to squeeze out of your life. Friendships may rarely be urgent, but in the long run, friendships just might save your life.

According to Harvard University professor and director of Harvard's Center for Population and Development Studies, Lisa Berkman, the quality of our relationships drives our health and well-being. In a study of 7,000 adults, those with fewer social ties were two to three times more likely to die during the nine years of the study than those who had plentiful relationships.[126]

Berkman's conclusions about the negative effects of isolation—and the positive effects of friendships—on our physical and mental health are corroborated by numerous other studies. The most profound is a Harvard study that has tracked 724 men since 1938. Robert Waldinger, the study's current director, said in his recent TED Talk, "The clearest message that we get from this 75-year study is this: good relationships keep us happier and healthier. Period." Socially disconnected people are, according to Waldinger, "less happy, their health declines earlier in midlife, their brain functioning declines sooner, and they live shorter lives than people who are not lonely."[127]

Berkman's research has also shown that good relationships boost "the immune system, speed recovery from surgery, sustain mental function in old age, and minimize the risk of anxiety and depression."[128] A meta-study of 148 studies with over 300,000 participants showed that "having weak social ties was as harmful to health as being an alcoholic, and twice as harmful as obesity." One of the co-authors went so far as to say, "a lack of social relationships was the equivalent of smoking 15 cigarettes a day."[129]

In an article for *The New York Times,* Dr. Dhruv Khullar of Massachusetts General Hospital and Harvard Medical School addresses the issue of social isolation and health head-on. "Loneliness is as important a risk factor for early death as obesity and smoking," says Khullar. This data is even more alarming when we consider that social isolation is a growing epidemic. Since the 1980s, "the number of American adults who say they're lonely has doubled from 20 percent to 40 percent. A great paradox of our hyper-connected digital age is that we seem to be drifting apart."[130]

Khullar then goes on to cite a series of data, each item more alarming than the one before. One-third of Americans older than 65 now live alone. Individuals with less social connection sleep worse, have poorer immune systems, and experience more inflammation and higher levels of stress hormones. He cites data pooled from 70 studies and 3.4 million people showing that socially isolated individuals had a 30 percent higher risk of dying in the next seven years, and the effect is largest in middle age.

And it is not just older people. Socially isolated children have been shown to have significantly poorer health 20 years later than children who have good social connections. When physicians are sounding the alarm over the health importance of our social lives, it's time to pay attention.

"Human connection lies at the heart of human well-being," Dr. Khullar says at the end of his startling article. But what kind of connection?

FaceTime™ vs. Face Time

Dhruv Khullar calls it a paradox that we are drifting apart in this hyper-connected age. What is this paradox about? How is it that we are sending and receiving billions of texts, emails, Facebook posts, tweets, and Instagram images—and yet we are simultaneously becoming less and less connected? It is quite simply, because those digital interactions aren't equivalent to good, old-fashioned, in-person relationships.

We may be gaining digital communities, but we're losing our neighbors and our in-person friendships, and it is hurting us. We need less work and digital time and more social, person-to-person time. To make that happen, we need to take a break from our devices and our busy schedules, and be proactive about connecting with people in the real world.

It is not a matter of just *having* friends. The frequency with which you *see* your friends is what matters most. The busier you are, the easier it is to let friendships waste away. Living a satisfied, full, and happy life is very hard to do without good friendships. This is where the Sabbath comes in. Everything that pushes friends away during the week—work commitments, emails, conference calls, business dinners—are all gone on the Sabbath. You have a whole day to yourself, your family, and your valued friends.

To keep friendships strong, it is important to spend time face to face. Social media and texting connect us and help us stay in touch, but they are no substitute for being in the same room with someone. Technology just can't deliver the same satisfaction and happiness. A survey of 5,000 Canadians showed that "online friends have zero effect on well-being." It didn't matter how small or large your group of online friends were, there was no effect.[131] Compare this to research Khullar cites showing the strong positive effect real-life friends have on well-being. Don't get me wrong; using FaceTime and Skype to communicate with friends and family is a true marvel, particularly if your loved ones are far away. It is better than no contact at all, but it is no substitute for being in the same place with them.

Between work, your spouse, and your children, it can be hard to carve out time during the week for your friends. In my experience, having an extra day where you can simply hang out with friends—with little or no time pressure–is pure heaven.

And since time is not a renewable resource, this extra time has real value. There is no such thing as "free time." We may not be occupied or have a task to do at the moment, so we think we have free time, but that time is always worth something to us or to others. Time slips from our grasp every second of every day. It is finite and precious. You can get a new job, make more money, or busy yourself with countless activities, but you never get back the time you spent or lost. As one of the richest men in the world, Warren Buffett, has said, "Money has no utility to me. Time has utility to me."[132]

Time vs. Money

Life often forces us to choose between money and time. Do we spend more time earning more money or do we spend more time relaxing and connecting with friends and family? Aside from the satisfaction and joy you get from work and having a successful career, what is the value of your time? What is time with your family worth? What is a happy life worth...a happy marriage...time with friends?

A recent University of California, Los Angeles survey showed that 64 percent of Americans say they would choose money over happiness.[133] Study after study, however, has shown that happiness is greater for those who choose time over money. The studies' results held true even when adjusted for income level, marital status, and gender. Unfortunately, for many Americans, there is no choice. They must choose money because of their financial situation or other responsibilities. Due to substantial debts, health care costs, or some other situation that is life-or-death, some people have to spend the vast majority of their waking hours working. Even for these people, there are aspects of the Sabbath to integrate into daily life. Regardless of your situation, it is still possible to make even small choices based on an understanding of the toll technology can take on you, the importance of social ties, and the value of letting your brain rest. You can still squeeze in time for smaller hard breaks. When you don't need your phone, turn it off. Share meals with loved ones when you can, with no distractions. Even these small moments can decrease your stress and enrich your life.

Research indicates that in the U.S., income is positively correlated to happiness up to about $75,000 a year. That means for people with incomes from zero to $75,000 a year, the more money you make, the happier you are likely to become. Above that $75,000 level, the correlation weakens substantially, which means that there isn't a proportionate increase in happiness as you make more money.

Consider that between 1957 and 1990, per-person income in the United States doubled, net of inflation. Not only did reported levels of happiness fail to increase at all during the same period, the rate of depression grew nearly tenfold. The incidence of divorce more than doubled, while cases of suicide, alcoholism, and drug abuse also rose dramatically.[134, 135, 136]

Money does not equal happiness. That is something everyone understands— at least, everyone making more than $75,000 should understand this.

We can't replace time and it is arguably our most valuable asset. We couldn't get even get one second back if we tried. So why do we treat it as an inexhaustible resource that is easily renewable? Why don't we treat it as one of the most valuable things we control?

In Matthew Sleeth's book on the Sabbath, *24/6,* he says, "One day a week adds up. Fifty-two days a year times an average lifespan is equal to more than eleven years."[137] Imagine giving yourself eleven full years of joy and satisfaction that also happen to improve your health, your work, and the quality of your life.

The effect of the taking one day off isn't that something magical happens on any one Sabbath, it's that a cumulative positive change occurs over time. For at least one day, I get to control my time and possibly add years to my life, and they will be the best years possible, filled with happiness, health, friends, and family.

CHAPTER 16
RITUALS' REWARD

Our purpose and values are like a rope that runs through our life
and that we must keep ahold of day in and day out.
Rituals of remembrance help us keep our grip on that rope
through life's dark tunnels.

—BRETT AND KATE MCKAY, "THE POWER OF RITUAL"

Former Boston Red Sox third baseman Wade Boggs was infamous for his pre-game rituals. He woke up at the same time each day, ate chicken before each game, took exactly 117 ground balls in practice, took batting practice at 5:17 p.m. exactly, and ran sprints at 7:17 p.m. exactly. Boggs also wrote the Hebrew word *Chai* ("living") in the dirt before each at-bat, even though he was not Jewish.[139]

Completely silly and ridiculous, right? The problem is that Wade Boggs is not only in the Baseball Hall of Fame, but is also considered one of the top 100 individuals ever to have played the game. Who are we to say his rituals were crazy, or that they didn't work?

Rituals have been with us for thousands of years, and they vary across religions, cultures, and societies. From how people start their day to the way they pray and memorialize their dead, rituals come in all shapes and sizes.

The Mental and Physical Health Benefits of Ritual

Research tells an interesting story as to why rituals exist. They exist because they work. In high-pressure tasks, anxiety can be lowered and confidence increased through the use of rituals. After the death of a loved one, rituals reduce the suffering of those in mourning. Rituals can even affect our enjoyment of life. Studies from Harvard have shown that chocolate, lemonade, and even carrots taste better when consumed as part of a ritual![140]

Researchers at the University of Minnesota and Harvard found that "families that consistently enact ritual behaviors have children with better self-control and academic performance than families that do not make use of rituals."[141]

To summarize: rituals can lower anxiety and increase confidence in stressful situations, reduce suffering after the death of a loved one, increase the enjoyment of food, and provide significant benefits to the lives of your children—and those are just the results from a handful of studies. It almost sounds too good to be true, but it isn't.

Why aren't we adding more of them into our lives? Think of the rituals that bring us happiness, meaning, and joy: weddings, bar mitzvahs, confirmations, and holidays like Thanksgiving, Passover, and Christmas.

So why not take on a ritual on a more frequent basis? We know that frequency is a key factor in promoting happiness. From attending religious services, to exercising, to visiting with friends, those who do it more frequently are happier. [142] There is a well-known psychological phenomenon called the "hedonic treadmill." When humans enter a new situation that they feel strongly positive or strongly negative about, their tendency over time is to normalize it, so that after a while, they cease to have strong positive or negative feelings about the situation. So, if we win a prize or the lottery, in the short run, we experience a surge in happiness, but in the long run, we become accustomed to our new circumstances and find that we are no happier than we were before. A similar thing occurs with people who are paralyzed in accidents: they tend to eventually return to a level of happiness only slightly below the level they were at before the accident. This phenomenon suggests that major positive events are not so reliable as sources of long-term happiness. What if, instead, minor events were the key to increasing long-term happiness?

Researchers have found that regular, reliable small boosts to well-being end up sustaining people and create cumulative long-term change. Harvard researchers found this to be true not only for people attending religious services, but also for people who exercise regularly.

On a weekly basis, the Sabbath ritual provides this small, regular boost. The powerful combination of benefits includes: reduced anxiety thanks to less scheduled activity; renewal and confidence derived from stepping away from the frenetic pace of daily life; and greater enjoyment thanks to having the time to savor meals and see the people in your life who mean the most– your family and friends.

The Story of Rachel

Sam Chafetz learned the true value of rituals from his daughter Rachel. Before she was born, Chafetz was a Harvard Law School graduate working for a prominent law firm in New York. He told me that he "never saw the daylight except through a window"–he was working that hard. So, in 1973, when he got the opportunity to return to his native Memphis to serve as in-house counsel for a prominent company, he jumped at the chance.

Unfortunately, that company went bankrupt in 1974. Then Chafetz's second child, Rachel, was born with a rare genetic disorder called ML4. When Rachel was only nine months old, Chafetz was told she would never be able to talk or see, and probably would not progress beyond the mental capacity of a two- or three-year-old. He and his family wanted to "dig a hole, jump in, and cover it with dirt."

He reached out to a local rabbi named Raphael Grossman for counseling. Grossman had lost a daughter at age 18 to leukemia, and Chafetz felt the rabbi could understand what he and his family were going through. The rabbi counseled them, and challenged Chafetz to come to synagogue and to bring his whole family.

"Why don't you come to shul (synagogue) for solace?" the rabbi asked. With nowhere else to turn, Chafetz and his family drove to the synagogue one Sabbath day. From the moment they entered, congregants hugged and pressed around Rachel, commenting on her lovely dress and engaging her as no strangers ever had. Instead of an awkward experience, the welcome they received changed their lives, and they eventually became an observant Orthodox Jewish family.

This meant that they went to synagogue every Saturday. Every morning, as she got older, Rachel would lift her fingers up in the air and have her parents count for her how many days were left until the Sabbath. That is how much that day meant to her. A girl who couldn't see or talk was able to communicate her connection to a special day when a community of people showered her with love and affection. Through Rachel, Chafetz realized the value of being part of a loving community that was created and solidified by the weekly gatherings.

Over the years, he has noticed that on the Sabbath, people talk about values and things that are meaningful–things like how to be a better person. On the other hand, Chafetz says, "Work is a means to an end, and I say that while acknowledging that I love what I do." Chafetz is now a prominent attorney who works in mergers and acquisitions at a Memphis firm with 850 lawyers. I connected with him through another CEO who had heard I was writing this book, and told me I had to talk to this fantastic lawyer in Memphis who is only "available to clients 24 hours a day, six days a week." Chafetz told me that he has never had a transaction fail because of his day of rest on Saturday. Many colleagues have told him they wished they could have a Sabbath.

One Sabbath story sticks out for Chafetz. He was working one Friday on a public offering when he discovered that one of the principals–none other than the CEO and founder–had been lying. Chafetz's client was the largest investor in the firm in question, and he counseled his client to fire the CEO. The day ended, and Sabbath began. Chafetz put his work aside to spend time with his family and pray at his synagogue. The next afternoon, there was a knock at his door. Four of his law partners had come to talk about the drama with one of the firm's biggest and most important clients. Since they knew that Chafetz didn't talk business on Saturday, they didn't discuss the specifics of the case. Instead, they had a conversation about principles and morality. "We had a conversation about how you prevent yourself from being a prostitute," Chafetz recalled. On Monday, the client fired the CEO.

The temptation in the business world is to look the other way, push things through, try not to make waves. It can be hard to be ethical and stand on principles, and to decide what is the right thing to do.

Chafetz's morality, strength, and confidence are informed by his observance of the Sabbath, something he learned to love through his daughter and the powerful effect of the ritual on her life. Two years ago, Rachel passed away. "She was a profound influence on her family and community," Chafetz explained. May we all learn to be the blessing that Rachel was to her family and community.

CHAPTER 17

THE SABBATH IS CHICK-FIL-A'S KEYSTONE HABIT

Keystone habits say that success doesn't depend on getting
every single thing right, but instead relies on identifying a few
key priorities and fashioning them into powerful levers.
—CHARLES DUHIGG, *THE POWER OF HABIT*

Remember from Chapter 14 that your brain uses a disproportionate amount of energy relative to its size. Habits emerge out of your brain's desire to conserve energy. In his wonderful and insightful book, *The Power of Habit*, *New York Times* reporter Charles Duhigg explains that when a habit emerges, your brain stops fully participating in decision-making. When a task has become habitual, your brain does not need to focus as intently on it, so it can divert focus to other tasks. Unless you deliberately fight a habit, this pattern will unfold automatically.[143]

The Power of Keystone Habits

Whether we realize it or not, for better or worse, habits dominate our lives. From brushing our teeth to exercise, a great deal depends on the habits we keep. Much of the time we are on autopilot, due to the brain's built-in desire to conserve energy.

Duhigg's book dives into how habits are formed, and the process of replacing bad habits and creating new ones. It contains fascinating stories and lessons, ranging from the habits of alcoholics to the ways habits galvanized support for civil rights icon Rosa Parks, to the transformative changes former CEO Paul O'Neill introduced at the Aluminum Company of America. In the Rosa Parks example, Duhigg shows us the power and value of social habits. Many other people were arrested for sitting in the wrong seat before Rosa Parks. Why did things change with her arrest? Duhigg argues that Rosa Parks had "a large, diverse and connected set of friends." The Montgomery bus boycott became a "society-wide action because of the sense of obligation" felt by her large number of friends. And it wasn't only Rosa Parks' direct friends who changed the course of history, but the friends of those friends. All of these people were acting on a certain kind of habitual behavior: when your friends need you, you jump in (yet another reason to invest in your personal friendships!)[144]

The most interesting part of the book for me was the idea of keystone habits. The keystone is the central stone at the summit of an arch that locks everything together. The rest of the stones are held together by the keystone.[145] A keystone habit is a habit that other habits depend on. Duhigg says that some habits matter more than others when we set about re-making our businesses and our lives. These keystone habits can influence how people work, eat, play, live, spend, and communicate. Keystone habits start a process that, over time, transforms everything.[146]

Duhigg says, "Keystone habits offer what is known within academic literature as small wins. They help other habits flourish by creating new structures, and they establish cultures where change becomes contagious. Small wins fuel transformative changes by leveraging tiny advancements into patterns that convince people that bigger achievements are within reach."[147]

How a 'Crazy Hippie' Used a Keystone Habit to Turn a Corporation Around

One story Duhigg tells in the book to illustrate the transformative power of keystone habits is that of Paul O'Neill and the Aluminum Company of America, or Alcoa, as it is better known.[148] When O'Neill joined Alcoa as CEO in 1987, the company was beset with labor strife, financial troubles, and a problematic safety record. In his first speech to investors and stock analysts, O'Neill didn't talk about profit margins, the labor difficulties, or new markets. He talked only about safety. He said, "I intend to make Alcoa the safest company in America." That was it. A few investors raised their hands to ask about inventories or capital ratios. "I'm not certain you heard me," O'Neill said. "If you want to understand how Alcoa is doing, you need to look at our workplace safety figures."

Investors were flabbergasted. One investor Duhigg interviewed reports running to a pay phone in the lobby (this was 1987–no mobile phones) and calling his 20 biggest clients, telling them, "The board put a crazy hippie in charge, and he's going to kill the company," and urging them to sell their stock immediately before everyone else did the same.

"I knew I had to transform Alcoa," O'Neill told Duhigg. "But you can't order people to change. That's not how the brain works. So, I decided I was going to start by focusing on one thing. If I could start disrupting the habits around one thing, it would spread throughout the entire company."

And that is exactly what happened. How? Here's an example: after one worker was tragically killed when he tried to fix a jammed machine by himself, O'Neill instituted a number of new safety policies, including that any worker could suggest new safety rules to management. One worker had an idea, not for a safety rule, but for how the company could respond much more nimbly to consumers' ever-changing preferences in aluminum siding paint colors. Within a year, Alcoa's profits on aluminum siding doubled.

It turned out that that worker had voiced that idea many times before, but had never spoken about it to management. As Duhigg explains, "Establishing an organizational habit of suggesting safety improvements had created other habits, as well: recommending business improvements that otherwise would have remained out of sight. By shifting worker safety habits, O'Neill had created patterns of better communication. A chain reaction started that lifted profits."

By the time O'Neill stepped down from Alcoa in 2000 to run the U.S. Department of the Treasury, Alcoa's annual net income had quintupled. Not to mention, the annual number of days lost to injury had dropped from 1.86 days to 0.2 days per 100 workers. As for that investor who told his clients to sell their Alcoa stock in 1987, he said to Duhigg, "It was literally the worst piece of advice I gave in my entire career."

I believe that just as safety represented a keystone habit that transformed Alcoa, so observation of the Sabbath is a keystone habit that will transform your life. I've seen this happen in my own life and in the lives of others, some of whom are profiled in this book. I believe that the hard break of a Sabbath results in small incremental improvements in our lives that bolster us every other day of the week.

Could turning off your phone and email for the Sabbath be one of these small wins? For me, it has been. The experience of being present without distractions during the Sabbath led me to realize how important it is to be present for people I care about at other times, too. So, I began putting away my cell phone when I was eating meals with family or friends on weekdays. When my phone is not on the table while I'm sharing a meal with loved ones, or when I put it on silent, there is nothing to distract me. I become more present, and I don't just listen, but I really hear what everyone is saying.

Another small win for me was that the Sabbath helped me create a weekly habit and ritual of calling my parents and brothers. Without the Sabbath ritual, I would not have realized that I wasn't communicating with them as much as I really wanted to, and how important it was to reach out to them. My relationships are stronger because of this weekly ritual. I'm more attuned to the ups and downs in my family's life than I was before. I can hear differences in their voices that alert me to things to worry about, or the need to check in more often during a given week.

Those are just two small examples. Other, larger ones include trying meditation and self-exploration because the Sabbath gave me the space and time to do so. When I lived in Atlanta, I took courses in CBCT (Cognitively-Based Compassion Training) meditation through the Emory-Tibet partnership at Emory University. The Sabbath also led me to learn more about my Jewish tradition, and that study has given me great satisfaction and deeper insight into my life and the lives of my ancestors. Not to mention that it was a Jewish learning retreat where I met my wife, who is truly my partner in all things: confidante, best friend, advisor, and mother all wrapped in one. She brings out the best in me, and the Sabbath is a time I make sure to reconnect with her. Brad Feld says one of the main reasons he takes a digital Sabbath is to spend quality time with his wife, who is his "favorite person on the planet." I, too, want to spend attentive time with my favorite person.

Because you slowly but surely improve your life on your Sabbath break, observing the Sabbath leads to better behavior throughout the rest of the week. The positive changes in your life build cumulatively over time.

How Chick-fil-A Succeeds by Closing Its Doors

One great example of how observing the Sabbath can become a keystone habit with a huge return on investment can be found at Chick-fil-A, an Atlanta-based national fast-food chain. Every week, all of Chick-fil-A's more than 2,000 locations are closed on Sunday.[149]

The founder, S. Truett Cathy, a devout Christian, opened his first restaurant in 1946. By the time Sunday rolled around, he was exhausted, and decided to close the store. The founder's son and current CEO, Dan Cathy, tells the story of his father and that first Sunday: "He figured if he didn't like working on Sundays, that other people didn't, either. He said, 'I don't want to ask people to do what I am not willing to do myself.'"[150]

Over time, Chick-fil-A stuck to their policy of being closed on Sundays, even as the world changed and the competition started opening every day.

The company came to believe that a mainstay of their business was closing every Sunday for the Sabbath. In conversations with me, executives at the company have told me that this keystone habit lets their employees know that every week, they have a day off to be with family and friends, and to spend time on their spiritual life, if they want. One of the company's core beliefs is that closing on Sundays, they experience less turnover, attract better employees who are more engaged, and offer better customer service.

Is it possible that Chick-fil-A is correct? Can you be more successful by being closed every seventh day? We know from research how detrimental it is for a person to work every day, but just how beneficial can it be for an entire company to take one day a week off, every week?

The answer is pretty clear. Chick-fil-A doesn't just beat their competition; they trounce them. They have the highest revenue per store of any fast-food chain in the nation, with the average store posting $3.9 million in annual revenue. Their nearest competitor is Jason's Deli, with $2.7 million. McDonald's is third, at $2.4 million. Their biggest competitor in the chicken fast-food space is KFC, which clocks in at $960,000,000 almost $3 million less per year per store. And keep in mind that KFC is open seven days a week![51]

If ever there were a business case for the Sabbath, Chick-fil-A is living and breathing it. Chick-fil-A's leaders believe that other benefits cascade off of the company's Sabbath policy. The Sabbath policy is founded in the belief that the company will thrive when people come first. It goes something like this: they want their employees to have a day off to be with their families; the employees genuinely feel cared for, so the company attracts and retains the best people, who then offer the best service; and customers love great service. Chick-fil-A scores the highest customer-service ratings in the industry, and the best customer-service and politeness ranking for a drive-thru restaurant.[152]

And there's more to the cascade effect. Caring for their employees via the Sabbath led management to wonder what else they could do to benefit their people. They realized that most of their employees were seasonal, and often in college or on their way to college from high school. So, they started a generous college scholarship program for employees. In 2017, Chick-fil-A estimates they awarded nearly $5 million, in the form of 1,850 scholarships.[153] Since 1973, more than 36,000 employees have received college scholarships from Chick-fil-A.

The company's corporate staff-retention rate has hovered at 95 to 97 percent since 1946. [154] In reviews of Chick-fil-A on Glassdoor, employees give the company an average of 3.9 out of 5 stars. Seventy-six percent say they would recommend the company to a friend, and 94 percent approve of the CEO. Compare that to chief competitor KFC, with its 3.2 rating, in which only 47 percent say they would recommend KFC to a friend, and only 59 percent approve of the CEO. [155, 156]

Another channel of the cascade: care for employees led the company to start caring more about the quality of the food, which led them to look more care-fully at how to raise the chickens they serve. Chick-fil-A announced that by 2019, it will only offer chicken raised without antibiotics. They are the only chain to do so. The company followed up that announcement in 2016 by committing to only serve 100 percent cage-free chickens and eggs by 2026.[157]

Chick-fil-A executive John Stephenson told me his customers and employees realize that "If Chick-fil-A stands firm on the Sabbath principle, then they are going to stand firm on cleanliness and good service. This adherence to standards and principles subconsciously translates into delivering an outstanding level of quality."

All of this clearly results in a company that is better in a multitude of ways. What started as a practice of closing on Sundays has turned into a keystone habit, a foundational principle of the company, and a big ingredient in its success. Chick-fil-A's sales have grown by more than 10 percent every year since 1946. And it has all been driven by a culture that rests solidly on the Sabbath.

S. Truett Cathy, who passed away in 2014, credited "blessings from the Lord" for the great success his company has enjoyed, and while alive, he remained as committed as ever to maintaining the closed-on-Sunday policy. He said, "I feel it's the best business decision I ever made."[158]

CHAPTER 18

THE SABBATH WORKS

Truth is what works.

—WILLIAM JAMES

I believe the Sabbath is a very powerful solution to the problems of successfully conducting business in the modern day—an ancient traditional day of rest from work. Why? I hope I've presented you with a great many reasons so far in this book but the number one reason I believe in the power of the Sabbath is: it worked for me. And it didn't just work. It transformed my life, both personally and professionally. The Sabbath has become special, even sacred, for me. It is my favorite time of every week. Others who take a Sabbath all speak from the same gospel, even those for whom the Sabbath has no religious meaning.

The value of a Sabbath is especially keen for those of us who are workaholics, driven to succeed in their field and accomplish many things. The Sabbath was made for people like me.

A Mormon Approach to Sabbath

It was also made for someone like Barrie Lindahl, who has never been in the office on a Sunday. His Sunday Sabbath is a time for family and church: The Church of the Latter-Day Saints. Not only is Lindahl not in the office on Sunday, no one else in his company is, either—just like Chick-fil-A.

One of Lindahl's companies is the Phoenix, Arizona-based Hub Realty Group, which owns 500 rental homes and manages another 1,500 for investors. In addition, Lindahl founded a company called Higley House that builds 600 single-family rental homes a year and sells them to investors. A new startup Lindahl is running is called SIBI, helping builders and landlords order appliances and flooring directly from suppliers. And if that's not enough, he builds furniture from specialty woods in his spare time.

"I could not imagine working on Sunday. It would be like running a constant marathon. I would not have the time to ponder and think," he told me. "I work 5:45 a.m. to 7:00 p.m. most days, and I even work on vacation." Lindahl's six-day-a-week regimen would sound exhausting to most people, but just the thought of working seven days a week is exhausting to Lindahl.

Starting on Saturday night, Lindahl turns off. His preparation for the Sabbath starts with a Saturday date night with his wife. This ritual helps re-connect him to the most important person in his life, and kicks off his Sabbath experience. "If I am out with my wife on any other day besides Saturday night or Sunday and my phone rings, I will take the call. But on Saturday night or Sunday, that will not happen," he said. More importantly, his wife knows it. "Sunday is the day to connect with my wife; touching and holding her." And this expectation is important, since Lindahl works so much the other days of the week.

He grew up in a strict orthodox Mormon family, so this is the world that he knows. "It's a habit, it's what I've done my entire life. It's the world I live in and the people I surround myself with," Lindahl said. Nevertheless, as he grew up, to make his Sabbath experience work, he created his own ground rules that differ from the traditional Mormon rules. For example, when he was growing up the pool was off-limits on Sunday, but Lindahl's family now hosts others for "family and friends" pool time. And while his rules may be more relaxed than the ones he grew up with, he does have hard-and-fast boundaries.

Lindahl's Sabbath rules include a family-first policy, three hours of church, and no hardcore activities such as hiking or skiing. He tries not to travel, and does not go to the grocery store or perform errands like getting the car washed. He hangs out with family and friends, has dinner with his extended family, and does not take business calls or check emails.

Having thought through his ground rules, Lindahl is better prepared for his Sabbath. His ground rules also communicate to his family, friends, and business colleagues what is most important in his life. That expectation is especially important to his family. They know that one day a week, they are the priority. His Sabbath experience is that much better for the preparation, thought, and expectations that go into the day before it starts.

An Orthodox Jewish Approach to Sabbath

Another driven, ambitious, and motivated person is former Senator Joseph Lieberman. If you were a U.S. senator and simultaneously running for vice president of the United States, it's safe to say you would have little free time on your hands. And yet from sundown on Friday till sundown on Saturday, Senator Lieberman did not campaign or do legislative work. "I have always been able to work harder on six days knowing that the seventh day of rest is coming," Lieberman writes in his wonderful book, *The Gift of Rest.*[159] He wonders how it would even be possible to do his job if he didn't take one day off.[160]

Just having the physical stamina to keep up with the demands of a nonstop news cycle, campaign donors, the media, constituents, and staff–not to mention family commitments–had to be overwhelming. The Sabbath has helped to sustain Lieberman's political career for 43 years, including the 24 years he served as a U.S. senator.

"Remember, I'm the guy with the personal custom of not wearing a watch on Shabbat so I can forget about the pressures of time, normally divided incessantly into fifteen- twenty- and thirty-minute blocks that go with my weekday job. The Sabbath is a welcome gift of rest and private time," he says.[161]

Politics is a profession of ego and power, and for Lieberman, this is where the Sabbath's magic comes in. One learns that the world will go on without them. The truth is that we–and the world–will survive just fine if we stop working or shopping, and stay at home with our families one day a week. "The fact is that none of us are essential every minute of the week can be humbling and anxiety-producing … but it is ultimately liberating," he says.[162] This comes from a man who has practiced politics at the highest levels, and works in a field where people take themselves incredibly seriously.

The Sabbath can bring moments of peace and relaxation, even in the most stressful of times. During the vote recount in Florida following the bitterly-fought election between Al Gore and George W. Bush in 2000, Lieberman and his wife shared a Shabbat dinner with the Gores. Remember, this was a moment when Gore and Lieberman were waiting to find out whether they would become president and vice president of one of the most powerful nations on earth—*after* the national election should already have decided it unequivocally. As orthodox Jews, the Liebermans naturally turned off their cell phones. Despite their eagerness to know what happened the instant that it happened, there came a moment when Tipper Gore turned to her husband and said, "Al, let's turn off our electronics. If anyone really needs us, they'll know how to get us."[163] Even with all the anguish, anticipation, and fear that permeated those stressful days, the Liebermans and the Gores were able to achieve some measure of peace and hope.[164] In moments of stress and tumult, the Sabbath is a refuge.

"Entering the Sabbath is like stepping into a different world," Lieberman explains.[165] He recounts another story, about American diplomat Richard Holbrooke, a relentlessly energetic and restless soul, who, after sharing a Shabbat meal with the Liebermans, was transformed. Lieberman was shocked to see how mellow and relaxed Holbrooke had become. "It was like Shabbat allowed Holbrooke to become a different person." Watching someone like Richard Holbrooke relax during a Sabbath meal convinced Lieberman that a Sabbath meal can change anyone. A different person is what the Sabbath beckons us to become.[166]

A Seventh-day Adventist Approach to Sabbath

Film producer and bestselling author DeVon Franklin is another powerful ambassador for the Sabbath.

Franklin was filming a pilot TV show for BET, and he was nervous. He is a Seventh-day Adventist, and observing the Sabbath is a cornerstone of his faith. The production of the reality show *College Hill* was "an all-hands-on-deck operation, and even if you were an executive, you had to pitch in." The problem was that "the shoot was going to happen after sundown on Friday, when I observe the Sabbath," he writes in *Produced by Faith,* his inspiring book about how to achieve worldly success arising from a strong foundation in faith.[167] The crew was short a cameraman, and they needed Franklin to handle the camera.

What was he going to do? He was a driven young executive, and the shoot was going to happen well into the Sabbath. He didn't want to let down the crew, but he didn't want to violate the traditions of his faith, either. He was torn, so he called his pastor, who asked him, "What do you value most?" He eventually decided to tell the crew he couldn't do the night shoot. And then he braced for blowback. And it never came. Everyone was cool with it, and several people even came forward to express curiosity about his faith and Sabbath practice.

Reconciling his faith with the demands of Hollywood was not easy at first. "But I have never given in. If I compromise on one Sabbath for one issue, then where do I draw the line?" he asks. "People in the business are surprised when I tell them I can't do something because of what I believe, but by doing so, I let them know what I value most. In an environment where everything is negotiable, taking something off the table and making it nonnegotiable can be empowering."[168] He decided not to take shortcuts. "If I want to be true to my beliefs, then shortcuts do not exist."

As an undergraduate at the University of Southern California, Franklin started as a lowly intern with Will Smith's production company. He then became a junior executive at Edmonds Entertainment, where he worked on *College Hill* among other projects. Through hard work and perseverance six days a week, Franklin rose to become a Sony creative executive, then moved on to senior vice president of Columbia Pictures, helping to turn the re-make of *Karate Kid* into an international success in 2010.

But during that movie's opening weekend, he had no idea if it was a success or not. The movie opened on a Friday, and remember, Seventh-day Adventists turn off their phones for the Sabbath from sundown Friday to sundown Saturday. So, it wasn't until Saturday night, when he turned on his phone, that he learned he had a huge hit.[169] This might seem like a counterintuitive way for a big-time studio executive to behave, but in reality, Franklin's keeping his phone off was not detrimental, either to the movie or to himself. By that point, there was no phone call, text, email, or social media post he could have made that would have substantially influenced the movie's box-office numbers. And his satisfaction at the movie's success was not diminished one iota by his finding out about it on Saturday night.

"If you make yourself all about work 24/7, your experience will be less rich, and your performance will suffer," Franklin says.[170] The joy and satisfaction that he gets from his work is enhanced by his Sabbath observance.

In 2014, Franklin started his own production company, Franklin Entertainment, which produced the faith-based hit *Miracles From Heaven*, starring Jennifer Garner and Queen Latifah. The movie cost $13 million to make, and went on to gross $73 million. With many other projects underway, the 39-year-old producer sees the Sabbath and his faith as the keys to his long-term success. "Sabbath actually makes me better at what I do," he said, "because it gives me one day to rest and recover from six days of working my crazy schedule so that I don't burn out."[171]

A No-Work Approach to Sabbath

As we have noted, overwork and burnout are extremely common in the tech startup world. Dan Shapiro, CEO of Glowforge, a 3D laser printing company, is part of a new generation of tech executives who are taking a more humane approach to work. Shapiro has taken a Sabbath since working at his first startup. "I could work long hours if I knew there was a safe space where I didn't have to work," he told me. In other words, by knowing there was a set period of time in which he didn't have to work, Shapiro found he could work harder.

He thinks the number one thing people do wrong when they start a new job or move to a new company is to entertain the idea that they must start by overworking, and can only ease up later. "Instead, they should set boundaries first," Shapiro says. "People have less respect for you if you start working one way and then change it later." It is much easier to be clear from the start when you will and will not work, and have people accept that. "I started [taking a Sabbath] when I started a new job early in my career. It is easier to do when you first meet people. People were curious, but no one questioned it," he said. This is a common observation among people I've talked to who take a Sabbath. No one seems to mind or question the practice. They just work around it. This has been true with me, as well.

When Shapiro started observing the Sabbath in 2003, he said, "It was the only boundary in my life at that time, and it was even more important early in my career." He has compiled an impressive resume. He started as a program manager at Microsoft, oversaw Games at Real Networks, then helped co-found the company that is now Photobucket. He founded a new company, Sparkbuy, which was acquired by Google, and then worked at Google for two years as CEO of Google Comparison, Inc. He wrote a book called *The Hot Seat: The CEO Guidebook,* created a board game called *Robot Turtles* to help preschoolers learn the basics of programming, and is now the CEO and cofounder of Glowforge.

Just looking at Shapiro's resume makes me feel unaccomplished. He is 42 years old, and has achieved all of this while taking one day off every week. That weekly recharge has helped him to be successful. For Shapiro, Sabbath is "avoiding anything work, anything that has to do with how I earn a living, though sometimes I lapse." Unlike the Liebermans or DeVon Franklin, Shapiro does not completely turn off technology; he just doesn't check email or respond to anything related to work.

This tactic has proven so powerful for him that he is implementing it at his company. The directive is not that everyone should do exactly what he does, but that each person should set individual boundaries that work for them. When people start working at Glowforge, they are encouraged "to create explicit expectations in terms of the hours they will be working." Shapiro's only stipulation is that employees be at the office from 10:00 a.m. to 5:00 p.m. from Monday through Friday so the company can operate effectively, especially with regard to communication during the workday. Beyond that, one person may decide to head home at 5:30 p.m. every day, and be offline from then on so they can make dinner and be with their kids. Another person may decide to take every Saturday or Sunday off from work.

Shapiro himself often goes home to spend time with his kids at 5:00 or 5:30 p.m., but once they are asleep, he might work until 3:00 a.m. "The fact that I'm at it until 3:00 a.m. may work for me, but not for you," he tells fellow employees.

Things have changed for Shapiro since 2003, when the once-a-week Sabbath was "the only boundary" he had in his life. Like others I have spoken with, the Sabbath has become a keystone habit for Shapiro, who has now integrated its principles into other times during the week. "The single greatest anguish in my life used to come at 5:00 p.m. every day. Do I go to a networking event, fundraise for my company, or go home and be with my family? This set up the need to trade family life for my job, or vice versa," he said. Now he creates a family time budget. He does not miss more than three dinners a week, and he will be out of town no more than three days a week. He has used the Sabbath as a keystone habit to extend the creative use of boundaries beyond the Sabbath itself.

Putting together Barrie Lindahl, Joseph Lieberman, DeVon Franklin, Dan Shapiro, Brian Scudamore of 1-800-GOT-JUNK? venture capitalist Brad Feld, and me, we now have seven case studies of business leaders from different industries, faiths, and walks of life, who all share the same passion for and commitment to the Sabbath, and who are all grateful for the role it has played in their success and happiness.

CHAPTER 19

BOSTON CONSULTING GROUP'S BIG EXPERIMENT PAYS OFF

The true method of knowledge is experiment.
—WILLIAM BLAKE

Perhaps the strongest proof of the value of the Sabbath comes not from an individual, but from the unlikeliest of places: the consulting industry. Consultants are expected to make work their priority, and are expected to be "always on." According to a recent Harvard study on consultants, nearly 50 percent of those surveyed said they worked more than 65 hours a week, not including the additional hours spent reviewing and responding to emails outside of work.[172]

By now, we know that work habits like these are not only unproductive and unhealthy, but are mainly for show. The leaders of Boston Consulting Group, sensing that their work culture was not healthy or productive, tried a counterintuitive experiment. In concert with Harvard University, they decided to see if giving selected consultants a predictable day off every week would improve their performance and engagement.

The Perils of Not Working Are Greatly Exaggerated

The experiment was led by Leslie Perlow, a Harvard professor of business leadership. In one part of the experiment Perlow and her colleagues devised, consultants had to take a day off in the middle of the week. In another part, they had to stop work–including email–every day at 6:00 p.m. "At first," she said, "the team resisted the experiment." The project leader became nervous at the thought of being forced to stop working and answering email. It took her six months to finally find a team of consultants at the firm who were willing to participate in the study.

These people were literally scared to stop working. "It's incredibly anxiety-provoking to turn off when you're not used to turning off," Perlow said. Some confided that they didn't think they would get promoted if they weren't seen as cranking it out and working long hours. One participant felt compelled to go around telling people he hadn't been laid off!

Perlow reported that in the beginning, "consultants ... either worked and felt guilty, because they were in violation of the experiment, or they didn't work and felt guilty, because of the stress they thought they were putting on their teammates."

Eventually, the anxiety and guilt subsided, and the consultants started to love their days and nights off. "I came back really refreshed," one reported. Over time, instead fearing that their careers would be damaged by participating, almost everyone in the firm wanted to be part of the experiment.

Participants in the time-off experiment reported higher job satisfaction, a greater desire to have a long-term career at the firm, and higher satisfaction with their "work/life balance." They also reported increased learning and development, and delivering a better product to their clients. Just as all the research and studies we've reviewed have told us, this real-life experiment showed that by taking a hard break from work, we improve both the quality of our lives and the quality of our work.

With predictable time off, teams started working smarter and reported more open communication with other teams. By backing each other up on days off, colleagues better understood their counterparts' jobs and needs. They also realized that maybe they didn't need overly long meetings, and could be more efficient with their time.

Boston Consulting Group is a behemoth in the consulting world, with more than 6,200 consultants, 12,000 employees, and annual revenues in excess of $5 billion. The senior leadership of the company wanted to create a durable company culture that would lead to more engaged employees, higher retention, and better quality of work. Based on the unequivocal success of this experiment, they made predictable time off an integral part of the company culture.

Boston Consulting now has a program called PTO, for Predictability, Teaming, and Open Communication. The program combines conventional "work/life balance" efforts with attempts to rethink work processes and make the work itself more meaningful. It has led to a 74 percent increase in reported intentions to stay at the company long term.[173]

There's another name for PTO, and it's been around for thousands of years. It's called the Sabbath.

"Look, I Don't Know Anything About Your Church..."

Corporate America is slowly starting to realize that the culture of the last 20 to 30 years is no longer working. Consider what Boston Consulting Group's corporate culture was like in the late 1970s. Harvard Business Professor Clayton Christensen tells a story about those times, when he was a newly-minted MBA and got a job at Boston Consulting:

> I had been there about a month when the project manager came to me and said, "Clay, we need to meet Sunday at 2:00 p.m., because we have a big client presentation on Monday, and we have to be sure everything is in place." I said, "Oh my gosh, Mike, I forgot to tell you. I'm a religious guy and I made a commitment that I wouldn't work on Sunday." And he just went bonkers: "Everybody here works on Sunday."

> "Well, I made a commitment that I wouldn't."
> "Look, I don't know anything about your church, but my church, if I need to do something a little bit shady, I just do it and then I find a priest and confess I did it, and promise to never do it again. Doesn't your church have some kind of escape like that?" I said, "I've been looking for that out, and haven't found it. I can't do it, I'm sorry."

So, he blustered away, and about an hour later, he comes back and says, "Look, Clay, I talked to everyone, and it's fine. We will meet on Saturday at 2:00 p.m." And I said, "Oh man, I forgot to tell you, I made a commitment to my wife that I wouldn't work on Saturdays." Mike went even more bonkers and said, "Look, Clay, whatever commitments you make to your wife about Saturday, just this once, with this extenuating circumstance, wouldn't it be okay to break it just this once?"

I told him that I wasn't on this earth to make the partners of BCG richer. I said, "I really want to be a good husband and a good father, but if I spend my Saturdays here at BCG, I will be implementing a strategy that I don't intend to pursue." And he was mad at that.

About an hour later, he came back and said, "Look, I talked to the team, and do you happen to work on Friday, perchance?"

Keep in mind that this is the same Boston Consulting Group that has now made it corporate policy for their employees to have predictable time off. This is the same company that now sees the benefit of a Sabbath and a hard break. Boston Consulting Group is now consistently ranked as one of the best companies to work for, coming in at number three on *Fortune's* annual list, and number one in *Consulting Magazine's* rankings.[175]

PART THREE

A

SUCCESSFUL

SABBATH

CHAPTER 20

THE SEVEN STEPS
TO A SUCCESSFUL
SABBATH

Success depends upon previous preparation,
and without such preparation there is sure to be failure.

—CONFUCIUS

Have I convinced you to take a Sabbath? Ready to try it, but wondering how to do it? Worried about turning the phone and email completely off and taking a true day of rest? Good. It's completely normal to be worried. I know I was when I started.

Below are seven steps I've identified as the key to creating a successful hard break or Sabbath. I encourage you to read through them now and take them in. Then, as you ready yourself for your own Sabbath, you can turn to the end of this book, where you will find a worksheet to facilitate your bold experiment in self-transformation.

1. **Prepare and Set Ground Rules**
2. **Take Baby Steps**
3. **Ritualize Your Sabbath**
4. **Have a Family Meal**
5. **Take a Walk in the Park**
6. **Make It Special**
7. **Spread the Message**

Prepare and Set Ground Rules

He who is best prepared can best serve his moment of inspiration.
—SAMUEL TAYLOR COLERIDGE

No matter how you decide to start, you need to set the ground rules that will govern your day off. Is it going to be a whole day, or just a morning or afternoon? Are you going to have any scheduled activities? What should you allow yourself to do and not do?

A lot of questions surround use of technology. For example, are you going to keep your phone completely off, or use it only for personal matters? If your phone is off, how will people get in touch with you? What if there is an emergency? How will you arrange to meet people during the Sabbath without a phone?

Just thinking about these questions might strike fear in your heart. So, take a deep breath, and remind yourself to operate from truth, not fear. The fact is, very little happens on Saturday or Sunday. If it is well prepared for, a 24-hour break should not impact anyone adversely. Very few emergencies need an immediate response. What about that nagging worry in the back of your head about responding to loads of emails? In my case, taking a day off energized me, and made me excited to tackle what I had missed. My curiosity easily overwhelmed any stress I felt. It will be all right!

Okay, so we've got one day a week. How do we catch up with our spouses and children and our friends, not to mention other relatives, like parents, uncles, cousins, or a sister who might live 40 miles away? And don't forget about time to relax and daydream, which we now understand is essential for creative thinking. How do we manage to do all of this on our one day out of seven without the Sabbath becoming another source of stress?

Let's take a deep breath, and remember that the goal is not to create another day jam-packed with things to accomplish and do. Also, remember that the Sabbath is a cumulative experience. Try picking one or two things (maximum) to do. You aren't supposed to try to accomplish everything on the Sabbath. Be more conscious of what you would like to do over the long term, not on any one day.

Remember, we can always modify any rules we create for a Sabbath, especially if they aren't working as hoped. Try to keep them, and jettison them only if they really aren't working.

It is not so hard to prepare yourself and others for your time away–your time disconnected. All my family, co-workers, clients, investors, and everyone else I deal with know that from Friday night to Saturday night, my phone is off, and I do not respond to emails. Everyone also knows that I will turn back on sometime Saturday night. So, as part of my advance preparation, I know that big decisions need to be made by Friday afternoon or delayed until Sunday or Monday.

Brian Scudamore and his team at 1-800-GOT-JUNK? have a nine-step process for when employees go on vacation. Brian and his team shared this process with me, and it is a great example of how to prepare before going dark. The steps include heavy communication with the team in advance, setting up automatic email and voicemail responses, and scheduling post-time-off catch-up time. The last step is to go dark. While preparing for one day off is not as extreme as preparing for a multi-day vacation, the more preparation and communication you do in advance, the more hassle-free the day or time will be.

Sometimes, it can be quite stressful to get ready for turning off and stopping all work activity. I've had several Friday afternoons that were full of frantic rushing, completing projects, sending emails, and having phone conversations while watching the clock tick away. Many Fridays, I struggle with this, and it can be very stressful even now, after years of practice and habit. But every time I completely turn off, a wave of relief washes over me. And I mean every time.

In *The Gift of Sabbath,* Joe Lieberman fully admits that preparing for the Sabbath can be hectic and stressful. There is a hard cutoff. The senator is just as addicted to his smartphone as the rest of us.[176] Turning it off is what marks the separation between a regular day and the Sabbath.

The senator and many other orthodox Jews greet the Sabbath as if they were greeting royalty. Hasidic Jews used to run out to greet the Sabbath like you would greet a queen or a bride. So the senator dresses up for the Sabbath, and helps to clean his house and set the table for an elegant meal. He even picks out a good book to read the next day.

When he was a senator, Lieberman had specific instructions for his staff[177] so they could get in touch with him in case of a national emergency (in the Jewish tradition, matters of life or death take precedence over any rules). A lot of thinking and planning went into figuring out what would constitute an emergency and cause him to violate the Sabbath.[178]

In my family, my wife does not have the sort of unhealthy relationship with her phone that I do, so she leaves her phone on. If there were an emergency, close family would be able to reach her, if necessary. Thankfully, this has never happened.

To meet with friends, I simply make plans like people did before cell phones. I know this is a big shocker, but before cell phones and texting, people used to meet at specific times and places that were determined in advance. If I travel by car, I bring along a turned-off cell phone, in case of an accident or other emergency. In 11 years, I have only had to turn it on once for a medical issue.

Another trick I've pulled out of my sleeve a few times is to switch cell phones with my wife. With none of my apps, messages, or emails, my wife's phone has allowed me to get directions to my destination or to call in case of an urgent matter. Recently, my wife and I switched phones so I could to stay in touch with her when she was very pregnant.

I put a lot of thought into my own personal list of Sabbath rules–what I would and would not do. This proved to be very helpful in curating the type of Sabbath experience I was looking for. Here is my list:

1. My cell phone is completely turned off from sundown Friday to sundown Saturday.
2. My computer is off, as well, so there is no access to email.
3. I try my best to not talk about business or politics.
4. I allow myself to watch TV, but nothing about business or politics.
5. I drive, but only to visit friends and family, or go to movies or concerts.
6. I try to do little or no shopping, but will eat out with family and friends.
7. I have at least one special meal, often on Friday night, with family and friends.

These are the broad strokes of how I try to separate my Sabbath from everything else. Sometimes, it is hard. For example, I try my best to not discuss work, but sometimes talk of business if it arises in conversations with others. If someone brings up business, politics, or money, I try to steer the conversation away from those topics, keep the conversation very short, or ask to continue it after the Sabbath is over.

An interesting thing happens when you make a deliberate effort to not discuss work. You quickly notice that all some people talk about is business. Work, work, work. People love talking about work. Even on days off, when we ask people how they are doing, they will describe their workweek. After an exhausting week, when I felt I like was drowning, a day of rest seemed like an oasis in the desert. This purposely walled-off time gave me the energy to keep going the following week. The last thing I wanted to do on that day off was talk about work.

You may struggle for other topics to talk about, and that's okay. I struggled with this for a while. But I have found that the challenge to discuss something besides business or politics makes me probe deeper in conversation to learn more about the person I'm talking to. I learn more about the people I'm with on the Sabbath simply because I'm not talking about my work life. When I talk about work, I tend to get too excited and can dominate a conversation, so the Sabbath has also made me a better listener. Some may be frightened to examine their lives outside of work, because work is all that they have. All the more reason for a day to contemplate what kind of life we are leading.

I enjoy reading obituaries. It may sound morbid, but I recommend reading the obituaries in your local newspaper for a week or two. You will notice interesting details about how people live their lives. An illuminating insight that I have gleaned is that the most boring part of any obituary is usually the subject's work history. It is more interesting to learn where people lived, how they lived, their passions, and who they left behind. I've never heard anyone at the end of their lives proclaim, "I wish I'd worked seven days a week when I was younger!" It is ironic that obituaries can provide motivation and inspiration to take a break from constantly talking about business.

The Sabbath is a time to remind us to discuss the things in life that are important, but not urgent: family life, spiritual beliefs, desires, non-work aspirations. There is so much more to life than your career, and taking a day to talk about subjects beyond work or politics will deepen you. By taking a day off from talking about work, you reduce the emotional energy that work requires and give yourself room to view work from a greater distance. This will ultimately improve both work conversations and work quality. When I do turn back on after my Sabbath break, I get excited to rejoin the fray, and look forward to the frantic pace of the workweek with a new energy.

Take Baby Steps

Don't look for the big, quick improvement.
Seek the small improvement, one day at a time.
That's the only way it happens—and when it happens, it lasts.
—JOHN WOODEN

Remember that at first, I tried to keep my phone off from the time I closed my eyes on Friday night until noon on Saturday. It was hard! But I built up to a full day over the course of a few months.

I'm glad I took baby steps. It was the best way to ease into something that appeared impossible. That way, I didn't feel like I was taking on something truly gargantuan. Some may prefer jumping into observation of the Sabbath with both feet, but I gradually spread my wings, and my observance has stood the test of time—over 11 years and counting.

Remember, research shows that small wins are the key to creating successful habits. That is another reason to start your Sabbath practice with baby steps. Charles Duhigg describes this in his book, *The Power of Habit*: "Small wins fuel transformative changes by leveraging tiny advantages into patterns that convince people that bigger achievements are within reach." Duhigg showed how Michael Phelps' coach Bob Bowman taught Phelps habits and routines that led to small, consistent improvements and wins, which then helped Phelps handle the pressure of competing at the highest levels. Bowman says that on race day, Phelps is just letting his habits take control. "When the race arrives, he's more than halfway through his plan and he's been victorious at every step. All the stretches went like planned. The warm-up laps were just like visualized. His headphones are playing exactly what he expected. The actual race is just another step in a pattern that started earlier that day and has nothing but victories. Winning is a natural extension," Bowman said.[179] Phelps, of course, used these small wins in practice and preparation to build the habits that would enable him to win more Olympic Gold Medals than anyone in history.

It's also important to remember that the goal is not perfection. This isn't a black-and-white, one-way-or-the-other sort of thing. It is a goal to strive for. Consider the CEO of Zillow, Spencer Rascoff. A few years ago, he set a New Year's resolution to not check emails on Saturdays. "The first year, I struggled to stick to it. I only succeeded five out of 52 weeks, which was nothing to write home about. The second year, I got 10, and in 2016, I was up to 20." Halfway through 2017, and he was email-free for almost 80 percent of his Saturdays. To an analytical person like Rascoff, tracking his progress was important. Even though he was only marginally successful at first, every little success showed him he could do it and that he was making progress.

Rascoff's Saturdays are now filled with family, "and they're invaluable to me," he says. These insights have led him to give permission to others in his company to disengage. He says, "If you want to create a balanced culture, you have to live and breathe balance, too." Rascoff is leading by example, because he knows that it will help his company as well as his employees. "When people have the space to recharge, they're happier, more productive, and more likely to come up with creative ideas that can't surface when they're heads-down," he says.[180] Sound familiar?

The Sabbath is meant to be a day of rest and relaxation, so try not to add a whole bunch of non-work activities. That can make you just as crazy as working. I try to keep scheduled activities to a maximum of one or two. The last thing I want is to be running from one social or personal engagement to another. Then all I've really done is replace the sort of activities that normally fill my working day with different ones. By stepping into a Sabbath habit with baby steps, you can counteract the natural urge to be busy for no other reason than to be busy.

Ritualize Your Sabbath

The human soul can always use a new tradition.
Sometimes we require them.
—PAT CONROY

Over the years, I have added little rituals to both my preparation for and my observance of the Sabbath. For example, before I shut off my phone on Friday afternoon, I call a set number of people to wish them "Shabbat Shalom," or a peaceful Sabbath. I call my parents, my brothers, and Rabbi Alvin Sugarman (the rabbi I mentioned at the beginning of the book); and I used to call Sylvia Glass, an adopted grandmother who lived until she was 102 years old and was a very important person to me.

I started this ritual of calling loved ones after I realized during my time at The American Home that I hadn't talked to my parents in two weeks, and one of my brothers in almost three weeks. I was very stressed out and overwhelmed at work. But my relationship to my family is important to me, and I felt compelled to do something, anything, to make sure so much time did not pass between at least brief conversations with them. Now, I'm guaranteed to talk to them, or leave a voicemail saying I'm thinking of them and wondering how their week was. This simple ritual has added enormously to the way I enter the experience of Shabbat. My phone calls have become my entrance into my Sabbath. I couldn't imagine starting my Sabbath without talking to my family now, and it's something I look forward to–a weekly small win that supports the bigger win of sustaining my Sabbath practice over the years. My family also knows to expect my calls. I always get a little thrill when they beat me to it and call me first on Friday. It's important to me that they know how much they mean to me, and this ritual helps let them know that.

Another ritual I've put in place is getting flowers for my wife. The Sabbath is meant to be special, and I want her to know how special she is to me. There are many weeks when I don't get the chance to do this, but I do it if I am able (see "baby steps," above).

Another of my rituals is the simple act of taking a nap. A powerful lesson from *The Power of Habit* is to reward yourself for maintaining your healthy habits, and my nap is one of my rewards on the Sabbath. For me, few things are better than taking a Sabbath nap. Napping for me is pure pleasure. Several very successful people were famous for taking naps, including Winston Churchill, Thomas Edison, Napoleon Bonaparte, and John F. Kennedy.[181] Research backs them up. Some studies show a nap can increase alertness by 100 percent, as well as improve mood, sensory perception, and overall health. [182] To put it in layman's terms … you feel great after a nap!

When you make your own rituals, and think about how you want to experience the day, you are better able to immerse yourself in the fullness of the Sabbath. And keep in mind that there are two very easy and powerful rituals that offer amazing benefits–a family meal and a walk.

Have a Family Meal

Nothing—not a conversation, not a handshake, not even a hug—
establishes friendship so forcefully as eating together.
—JONATHAN SAFARI FOER, *EATING ANIMALS*

When I'm in a rush during the week, I "panic eat." This is what I call wolfing down a meal as if I may never see another morsel of food. If I'm not panic eating because of time pressure, I'm probably unsuccessfully trying to do two other things while eating–such as reading the news and answering emails or talking on the phone.

One of my favorite rituals during my Sabbath is to simply enjoy a meal. I'm not in a rush, and while I may not eat as slowly as I probably should, the meals are much more relaxed. More importantly, I'm sitting down to eat with my family and friends.

Unfortunately, families are eating together less and less often. Yet children who eat dinner with their parents five or more days a week have less involvement with drugs and alcohol, eat healthier meals, perform better academically, and report feeling closer with their parents than children who do not, according to a study by the National Center on Addiction and Substance Abuse at Columbia University. [183]

Why is this? In my experience, when we eat together, we talk and connect. Topics and conversations arise that might not come up otherwise. Spending more intimate time with your family brings you all closer together. During the Sabbath, you can easily have at least one meal with your family, and it is guaranteed not to be rushed.

Millennials are starting to return to the concept of communal meals. Young people feel like they are missing out on something very powerful and profound, and they are right. I am on the board of the Moishe House Foundation, an international nonprofit organization that promotes community for young Jewish adults from ages 22 to 30. Moishe House subsidizes the cost of a larger house or apartment for three to four Jews in their 20s so they can host Jewish programming. There are over 100 Moishe Houses around the world, from New York City to Paris to Buenos Aires.

The key driver that has made Moishe House so successful is simply shared meals in someone's home. Almost 50,000 young Jews attended a Shabbat meal at Moishe Houses in 2016. The satisfaction and joy of eating among strangers and friends in an intimate setting is very powerful, and young people are clearly responding. Another organization, OneTable, also helps young Jews host Friday-night Shabbat dinners for other young Jews.

It's not just the nonprofit world that senses this opportunity. Startups are popping up to serve the untapped desire of the next generation to connect with friends and strangers over shared meals. Feastly is one such company, billing itself as an "Airbnb for foodies" that connects people who love to eat with people who love to cook and host. People are paying to eat with strangers in other people's homes. Another social dining organization, 10 Chairs NYC, was profiled in a recent *New York Times* article that reported people are paying $80 per meal and making long-lasting friendships with strangers through the program.[184]

These companies and non-profits are simply tapping into the unmet need of people wanting to share meals together. Chef, author, and TV personality

Anthony Bourdain says, "You can learn a lot about someone when you share a meal together."

We can certainly learn a lot about who Gary Sabin is by hearing him talk about how important meals with his family are, especially on the Sabbath. A devout Mormon, Sabin has devoted his life to family, church, and giving back. He made a personal decision while in Stanford Business School that his business career would not compromise his values.

"It's a joke," he told me. "People don't have to work every day. They can get everything they need accomplished in six days." Sabin should know. He built, led, and sold three multi-billion-dollar real investment trusts (REITs), including Excel Trust, which he sold to Blackstone for $2 billion in 2015.

Besides having an extremely successful business career, Sabin has been married for over 40 years and has five children. Despite the pressures of leading three large companies, he made sure never to work on Sunday. If business travels sometimes meant he had to be somewhere besides home on Sunday, he still would not work.

Family meals are so important to Sabin and his wife that they added a Monday-night family dinner to make sure the family ate together more than once a week. Sabin is convinced that "unpersuasive communication" is vitally important to children. For him, this means spending time just being with your children, and not telling them what to do. How can you learn who your children are if you don't have this kind of unstructured time? It's so much more than making sure they do their homework and aren't getting into trouble. Children learn by example, and having them observe how you choose to live your life and allocate your time is a great teaching tool.

While Sabin no longer leads a company as CEO, he has taken on a leadership role helping guide the Mormon Church in Europe. He and his wife moved to Frankfurt to help run the church's operations in over 39 countries. This latest job, which is a volunteer position, comes after founding and chairing the Sabin Children's Foundation, which addresses the serious medical needs of children in Africa, India, Central and South America, and the Philippines. He is an example not only to his children, but to us all.

Take a Walk in the Park

No man should go through life without once
experiencing healthy, even bored solitude in the wilderness,
finding himself, depending solely on himself and thereby
learning his true and hidden strength.

—JACK KEROUAC

The Sabbath is a great time to go for a walk, take a hike, go for a run, or ride your bike. Get outside. The benefits are enormous, including everything from preventing disease to strengthening your bones and muscles to improving your mood.

But where to go? How about out into nature? University of Michigan scientists have found that walking in the woods "significantly improved cognitive performance." The research did not find the same benefit from walking in an urban environment. The scientists theorized that the stress of walking amidst the urban hustle and bustle did not relax or calm people down.[185]

Stanford researchers have found that creativity can be boosted by 60 percent simply by going for a walk, while another study from the University of London shows a 50 percent increase in creativity and problem-solving ability.[186] Remember Albert Einstein's long walks without socks? Einstein joins Leonardo da Vinci, Ludwig van Beethoven, and Charles Darwin in the ranks of famously creative people who regularly took walks.

Steve Jobs, co-founder and former CEO of Apple, preferred to take a long walk while having a serious conversation, according to biographer Walter Isaacson. Mark Zuckerburg, the CEO and founder of Facebook, has taken up the practice, as well.[187]

If you are bored by the prospect of a simple walk, go for a strenuous hike. Studies have shown that hiking can reduce oxidative stress, which is thought to be an important factor in the onset, progression, and regression of cancer.[188] There is even a benefit to those who suffer from depression. And being in better cardiovascular shape offers a host of other rewards.

Rabbi Steve Cohen of Congregation B'nai B'rith, the reform temple I belong to in Santa Barbara, is a truly wonderful and amazing rabbi. I love his Saturday-morning Torah study, and I'm not alone; it is often overflowing. He combines intellectual rigor with great warmth, and makes a point of knowing in detail about the lives of people in our synagogue.

For him, the Sabbath is not what one would consider a day of rest. On Friday nights, he leads service from 5:30 pm or 6:00 pm until 8:00 pm, and socializes with congregants afterwards. And this follows a full day of work. On Saturdays, he leads a Torah study class at 9:00 a.m., followed by a Saturday-morning service that often includes a Bar or Bat Mitzvah, which runs until around 1:00 p.m. On Saturday afternoon, the rabbi may be able to settle in for some well-deserved rest, but it isn't exactly a relaxing day.

Everybody needs a hard break. If your job or duties in life dictate that you can't take off on the weekend, you can still create your own schedule–even if you are a rabbi. I asked Rabbi Cohen, since his Sabbath is so busy, what he does to take a break. It turns out his true Sabbath is Tuesday. His Tuesday tradition is to go out by himself in the mountains surrounding Santa Barbara and hike for five to six hours.

The stress of dealing with life, death, sickness, tragedies, joyous celebrations, teaching, and counseling can be overwhelming for any person in the clergy, no matter what their religion. Out there, he can he unload, process, and release the pressures of leading a congregation of more than two thousand people.

If you don't have a hiking or walking routine, it's not hard to create one. And remember the concept of small wins. We don't need to climb a mountain; it could be a walk around a neighborhood or city park. Start small, and build a lasting habit.

Make It Special

All of our sweetest hours fly fastest.
—VIRGIL

As I've made clear, on the Sabbath, I do place restrictions on what I do, especially around electronic devices. But my Sabbath experience is not ruled by what *I can't* do. On the contrary, it is governed by what I *can* do:

things like taking naps, going for walks or hikes, having family meals, or spending time playing with my children. I try to make it to study Torah at my synagogue, but with young children at home, I often cannot.

At home, I try, but don't always manage, to read something spiritual or philosophical. I read not only for meaning, but also for pleasure. Over the years, I have come to learn that I really love fiction. One of my favorite recent Sabbath memories is reading the bestselling science-fiction trilogy *Red Rising* by Pierce Brown. Having the time to spend on reading for pleasure is priceless to me.

In Hebrew, the word for holy is "kadesh." The literal translation of the word is "separate," not "holy." According to the Jewish tradition, the way you make something holy is to make it separate from everything else.

Rabbi and Torah scholar David Levin Kruss teaches that "most of the rabbis of the *Talmud* (the Jewish book of written laws) didn't believe that an object can be inherently holy. There are no magical objects. Only someone who brings the right intentions can create holiness. People create holiness, not the object itself, not even the day itself. People bring holiness to the day." On the side of his normal job of being an educator, he coaches people through the use of Torah learning. I normally study with him once a month, via Skype or FaceTime.

What you do during your Sabbath, should, ideally be different and separate from what you normally do. The point is to make it special, to infuse it with meaning and life. Start the process by thinking about your expectations and setting basic ground rules. Rabbi Kruss also says, "What makes something holy is the intention with which it is made and the use to which it is put."

The only way this hard break, this special day will work is through intention, thought, and separateness.

The best way to practice the Sabbath is to make it your own. Do what you normally don't do during the rest of your week. What is it that you don't get to do during your regular busy work days? What would make your hard break different, restful, and meaningful?

How about making love to your partner? According to Jewish tradition, it is mandated to have sexual relations with your partner on the Sabbath. In fact, in *The Gift of Rest,* Senator Lieberman discusses this very thing.[190] He relates a story of making his wife, Hadassah, blush at a Friday-afternoon campaign rally after being gone from her for a week, by saying, "I can't wait to spend the Sabbath with her." Most of the audience didn't know that in Orthodox tradition, that meant having sex, but she knew! To put it another way, this day should be about enjoying yourself as much as resting.

If, like me, you need to start with a period of time shorter than 24 hours, then by all means, do so. I also recommend working up to a full day. You'd be surprised how fast the time goes by. My wife used to joke that every Saturday afternoon, I would exclaim, "I feel great!" because it would take me until then to shake off the slings and arrows of the workweek. The time you need to get the full benefit of a break should not be underestimated. Sometimes, even a whole day doesn't suffice to relax me in body and mind. In general, I have found a full day once a week to be a reasonable balance between the demands of work and my own well-being.

New York Times op-ed writer Frank Bruni penned a wonderful essay in 2015 called "The Myth of Quality Time." Every year, Bruni and his extended family take a week-long vacation to spend time with one another. He confesses that when he was younger, he arrived late to the week-long gatherings or departed early, but says he now savors the whole thing from beginning to end, because "there's a better chance that I'll be around at the precise, random moment when one of my nephews drops his guard and solicits my advice about something private... Or when one of my siblings will flash back on an incident from our childhood that makes us laugh uncontrollably, and suddenly the cozy, happy chain of our love is cinched that much tighter."

He argues that we are less likely to have that kind of intimacy with short bursts of quality time. "We delude ourselves...that we can plan instances of extraordinary candor, plot episodes of exquisite tenderness, engineer intimacy in an appointed hour." In today's world, you can't really create those sorts of moments when everyone is frazzled and moving at the speed of light. Bruni writes, "People tend not to operate on cue. At least our moods and emotions don't. We reach out for help at odd points; we bloom at unpredictable ones. The surest way to see the brightest colors, or the darkest ones, is to be watching and waiting and ready for them."[191]

Worried about being bored with too much unscheduled time on your hands? A little bit of boredom, especially for kids, can be a good thing. A University of Colorado study found that "children who had more unstructured time and less time in formal after-school activities had stronger executive functioning."[192]

What will make the Sabbath special to us? Meditation, hiking, eating chocolate, listening to music, reading, volunteering—we know what makes our lives special, and it doesn't have to be something big. Spend some time thinking about it. With a little extra magic, the Sabbath will become precious to you.

Spread the Message

As we keep or break the Sabbath day, we nobly save or meanly lose the last best hope by which man rises.
—ABRAHAM LINCOLN

I think this is the most important step of all. After you integrate a hard break into your life, it is imperative to spread the message and fight the false messiah of extreme schedules, overwork, and busyness. How many of your friends and family are hurting themselves, their businesses, their loved ones, and their friends through destructive habits that are simply for show? Think of the value you can bring by sharing an ancient tool.

This sharing will not only strengthen your resolve; but if friends and family buy into the practice of taking hard breaks, it will immeasurably improve your Sabbath experience. You will be creating a community in which there are no worries about excessive schedules, interference from technology, or other distractions to diminish the Sabbath experience.

What are the best ways to spread the message? One is to lead by example. People will see your actions, and may decide to mimic what you do. They may start with small steps themselves. It's funny how the Sabbath is almost a counter cultural practice. It used to be a common part of the culture of our country. In 1849, President-elect Zachary Taylor refused to be inaugurated on March 4th, since that date fell on a Sunday, the Christian Sabbath. But nowadays, when you opt out of the 24/7 connected world, you stand out.

I've had a range of reactions to my own practice. The most common is curiosity. People are naturally curious when they encounter the Sabbath, and often want to know more.

Another important audience is our children. They watch our every move and repeat our words. As has been pointed out in this book, the risks for our kids of living a 24/7, always-on, connected life are even greater than they are for us. They have simply never known a world without the possibility of instant, 24/7 connection.

Another way to spread the message is to take issue with those who claim that the only way to succeed is to work ridiculous hours, burn out, and sacrifice everything at the altar of work. We can cite data, studies, and facts that clearly demonstrate overwork is bad for our health, productivity, and bottom line. Ironically, our higher levels of success, productivity, and work quality may be the ultimate way to spread the message, as the Boston Consulting Group has found.

One of my favorite people at The American Home was my chief operating officer, David Sullivan, who is now a good friend. He has since gone on to become entrepreneur in residence at Route 66 Ventures, an investment firm in the financial services sector, and is about to launch a startup called Till, a company that will offer renters rewards for paying rent on time or keeping their rental in good condition (think frequent-flier miles for renters). David is an exceptional guy, and was an extraordinary asset to TAH. He was also the kind of guy who prided himself on double espresso shots and working all-nighters. I really got worried about him in the final days of TAH—he seemed on the verge of completely burning out. Luckily, the sale of the company closed before that happened.

As much as I could, I talked to David about how important it was to take a hard break, how the world needed people like him, and how he needed to take care of his health. I'm happy to report that now, as he faces the challenge of launching a startup, David is a hard-break aficionado.

David told me, "A while back, I noticed a constant fatigue, being overwhelmed with a barrage of information." So, two months ago, he started a "work/phone Sabbath" from Friday night until Sunday morning. He's off the grid during that time, and describes the results as "transformative." He goes on to say:

> As an endurance athlete, I have learned over a decade that your body builds gains when it rests after activity. As my mental burnout became noticeable, I thought that I had been crazy to not implement a forced break from the constant deluge of information.
>
> A weekly detachment has allowed my brain to rest and reflect. I would argue my day off is my most productive day. Not only do I stay engaged with my family and friends, but it is becoming my most creative day. Being unplugged from inbound info and daily tasks required for progress gives my brain space to work in the background and generate ideas from quiet reflection. I keep a pad of paper around and will write ideas down as they come, but then quickly allow them to pass so I may stay engaged in whatever I am doing.

In other words, like creative people from Leonardo da Vinci to Kanye West, David has discovered the power and necessity of daydreaming for creative thought.

Reinforcing the idea of keystone habits and small wins we've discussed in this book, David says, "As I have come to appreciate the mental space, I have started trying to implement small breaks throughout the day. Transitions during the grind are great periods to reflect, shut my eyes, and breathe."

Old habits die hard. Like everyone else, David had become addicted to his phone, and found himself picking it up during his mini-breaks throughout the day. "What a terrible way to relax—to barrage yourself with social media, pictures, and news. Social media is the antithesis of relaxing. It's like having to do wind sprints between sets of lifting. Anyway, I've deleted all social media apps, and am noticeably happier and more relaxed."

I respect David so much that if he were a stock, I would buy him. Instead, I plan to invest in his new startup, which I feel all the more confident about because I know it's being run by a man who has hard breaks in place to manage the stress of startup life. It fills me with pride and satisfaction that I have been able to influence someone so talented, whom I respect a great deal. I'm pleased that I may take part in his success, both personally and professionally.

By spreading the message of the hard break, we also remind ourselves why we are taking a hard break, and of its importance in our lives. The value of the Sabbath for our loved ones is just too great for us to remain silent and accept the status quo.

THE SPACE FOR BIG QUESTIONS

He who has a Why to live for can bear almost any How.
—FRIEDRICH NIETZSCHE

Why Do We Work?

Harvard business professor Clayton Christensen has a front-row view of America's future business leaders. He said, "I look at the Harvard [Business School] students who graduate every year. Not a single one of them has a plan to go out and get divorced, or to raise kids who hate their guts."[194] And yet a shocking number of graduating students in business and other fields end up doing exactly that. Why?

The answer is that they invest only in the things that pay off fast. If you are the kind of person who has a high need for achievement, whenever you have an extra 30 minutes or ounce of energy, you subconsciously ask, "What could I do that will promote the most immediate and tangible sign that I have achieved something?" Careers provide these immediate, tangible signs of achievement: we close a deal, we ship a product, we get promoted, we get paid.

On the other hand, it is much harder to see immediate signs of achievement in our home lives. Our children misbehave every day. The house gets messy every day. So when we have a choice of how we will spend that extra ounce of energy, we invest it where we get the most immediate return. Unfortunately, for many of us, that is not at home.

Money doesn't bring happiness; we know that. We strive for it anyway, driven by the need for achievement. The Sabbath is your chance to focus on what is important in the long term, and to create a life with a principled foundation.

Why do we work? Why do we spend our time the way we do? Why do we keep ourselves so busy? These questions can only be answered when we give ourselves the time to reflect.

How can we become the best versions of ourselves? How can we realize all of our potential if we don't give ourselves the time and space to reflect and go deep into our inner lives? I don't think this is possible in a 24/7 world. Psychologist Tony Crabbe puts it best when he says, "The busyness of life, especially work and our stimulation devices, are helping us avoid doing the critical psychological work we need to do to become whole."[195]

"Who Shall Be Driven, and Who Shall Be Secure?"

Reminders of their own mortality often prompt people to reevaluate their lives. This was true for the late Randy Pausch, a computer science professor at Carnegie Mellon, who wrote a bestseller called *The Last Lecture* after finding out he had advanced pancreatic cancer. One of my favorite quotes from the book is, "Time is all you have. And you may find one day that you have less than you think." Randy learned this earlier than most.

Levi Felix, Brian Scudamore, Brad Feld, Jason Lengstorf, and Matt Auron are just a few of the people profiled in this book who experienced a mental or physical crisis. For that matter, so did I. We shouldn't need to wait for some stark reminder of mortality to make a life change. Life is short for all of us, and time is precious.

On the Jewish High Holidays of Rosh Hashanah and Yom Kippur, Jews recite an old prayer called *Unetaneh Tohkef.* This famous prayer starts out by saying, "On Rosh Hashanah it is written and on Yom Kippur it is sealed. Who shall live and who shall die?" Then it goes to list a bunch of ways one can die, such as "who by hunger and who by thirst." Another line near the end asks, "Who shall be driven and who shall be secure?"

At one point, when I was living in Atlanta and running The American Home, I started having chest pains. I decided to go to a doctor to rule out potential heart problems. Luckily, I happened to go to a wonderful doctor who took one look at me and saw a seriously stressed-out person on the road to poor health. This doctor happened to be Jewish, and he gave me a sermon that you might expect from a rabbi. He explained to me that each line of the *Unetaneh Tohkef* prayer compares opposites. He told me the opposite of being secure in life was being driven, and that what he saw before him was a person who was driven, and not in a healthy or productive way. He knew I was studying Judaism, and used that as a tool to it get through my thick skull that the always-worried, always-driven working lifestyle was not sustainable or desirable in the long run. As I've mentioned, at that point in my life I was already observing the Sabbath, and while my observance saved me from being even more stressed out than I was, clearly, the doctor was trying to tell me through his interpretation of the *Unetaneh Tohkef* that I still had more to learn about the value of rest. I have never forgotten his words.

Rabbi David Levin Kruss, upon hearing that story, told me that "the fragility of life and how it can change so quickly is the lesson of this prayer." As I get older, the lesson sinks in a little more. Friends and family members get sick; some die, others become permanently injured. The Sabbath is my way to make sure that I'm grounded and never forget.

More than a pause, more than a short break, the Sabbath invites us to contemplate and transform our lives. It's not just restful and refreshing, it is also an opportunity to make true and lasting change. It really all comes down to what we make of our time. Don't we want to carve out time that can elevate our reason for living?

Brett and Kate McKay, in a piece for *The Art of Manliness* blog, say it perfectly:

> Oftentimes, when we lament the flatness of our modern world, and wonder "Is this all there is?" we think, consciously or not, that the remedy will simply come into our lives. Or we think that there's nothing we can do about this listlessness anyway, so why bother? But like all good things, texture and meaning–a rich, multi-layered life–don't just happen. We create the texture and meaning by carving pockets of the sacred in the profane, by creating new structures for being inside different worlds of possibilities.[196]

This is the potential of the Sabbath. Beyond acting as a means to greater productivity, better health, a happier family life, and clearer work/non-work separation, the Sabbath can be the cornerstone that allows us to fully contemplate our lives. It can be as meaningful and as big as we want it to be.

What Will the Next Chapter of My Life Look Like?

I'm 12 years into my practice of the Sabbath, and I feel more connected to myself, my family, my community, and my God. Thanks to the Sabbath, I have been able to answer important questions about who I am, why I am working, and what is important to me. And that has made me stronger and more resilient than I have ever been in my life. I still struggle and have difficulty in my work and personal life. I still wrestle with my own workaholic issues and my addiction to my cell phone. But the Sabbath continues to offer me wisdom and equanimity that help me with my struggles, and through my practice, I'm stronger now than I have ever been. I'm writing this book not just for other people, but as an exercise in reminding myself of the effort I have to put in every day and every week to keep myself balanced and healthy.

My own practice will be especially important now that I am embarking upon a new adventure—an opportunity that has come my way just as I've been doing the final edits on this book. It began in 2016, when my friend Gabriel Halimi called me to say that he was starting a new company with his father. His father, Henry, a mechanical engineer, had been in the plumbing equipment business for 25 years, including stints as an expert witness when plumbing equipment companies got sued. An authority on fluid dynamics and plumbing, he wondered if a device could be invented to protect homeowners from leaks and water damage.

Over ten years, Gabriel's father developed a wifi-connected water valve that will not only detect leaks, but also allow a homeowner or building manager to shut off the water in a home by pressing a button on their phone. Not only that, but the device can learn what is normal and what isn't in a given home, and can shut the water off by itself when abnormal water flow is detected.

While I was running The American Home, if someone had asked me whether I wanted a device connected to each of my rental homes that alerted my maintenance staff of a leak or catastrophic pipe break, I would have said, "Sign me up!" So, I became an early investor in the company Gabriel and his father started, FLO Technologies. After two years and two rounds of fundraising, the company's first device launched in January of 2018.

In November of 2017, I called Gabe to see how things were going, and to get an update. Over the course of our conversation, I asked probing questions and shared hard-won insights from my time at The American Home. Suddenly, Gabe stopped mid-conversation and asked, "Aaron, would you ever consider joining our company?"

After two months of talks, I joined FLO as chief strategy officer, to assist in defining and implementing the company's strategy, take over business development and sales, help with the raising of capital, and oversee finances until a CFO can be hired. In other words, I'll be helping Gabe run the company, and do whatever he needs.

I'm excited because of the opportunity to solve the problem of water leaks, which vexes homeowners, landlords, insurance companies, and utilities, and hurts communities struggling with water.

I had some trepidation about joining the startup world again. I wondered, was I ready to once again jump off a cliff and build the airplane on the way down, as LinkedIn founder Reid Hoffman put it? Would the Sabbath be enough to protect me from the grind and intensity of what was to come? I worried about the time commitment, and had many conversations with my wife. Was the opportunity to work with my friend, who I respected so much, worth it? Was the thrill worth it? Would the financial rewards be enough to take me away from family and personal time?

I don't have all the answers to those questions. Time will tell. But I am excited to work with my friend, and to be in on the ground floor of what I consider to be an important product offering. I'm also very grateful that the Sabbath will be there to shelter and protect me from the rushing onslaught of the business world.

Based on hard lessons at The American Home, and all that writing this book has taught me about the importance of creating a humane company culture, I plan to bring my Hard Break/Sabbath philosophy to FLO. Can hard breaks help others in the organization? What will it mean to the future of the company? Will it make us stronger? I think so. Stay tuned to find out!

A Shelter from the Onslaught

My wish is that everyone will create regular hard breaks in their lives. I hope and trust that through hard breaks, other people's lives will be transformed as mine has been, and as others' have been before me. By taking a hard break and observing a Sabbath, we can live happier, healthier, stronger, more engaged, and more fulfilling lives.

Writing this book has been one of the hardest things I have ever done, but I find that when I'm passionate about something, I'm willing to go the extra mile and push myself. And this book has required a lot of pushing. Of course, taking a Sabbath helped me replenish myself for the challenging work of creating this book, too. My hope is to transform how we think about work, work culture, life, and technology—and to help us give ourselves a break from the modern world.

Thank you for taking time out of your busy and harried life to read this book. I would love to hear your comments, questions, and, of course, your stories. Please contact me at: aaron@thehardbreak.com.

No matter what, please make sure to build hard breaks into your life.

THE HARD BREAK
WORKSHEET

I have found that writing is a concentrated form of thinking, and writing down my beliefs and goals helps me to be clear about what I want, to live my beliefs, and to achieve my goals. So here I offer a set of questions and lists to facilitate your hard-break experience.

- **Section One** is an invitation to reflect on your life as it is now, and identify opportunities for change and growth that a hard break will enable.
- **Section Two** will help you set up the specific details of your hard break.
- **Section Three** will allow you assess your hard-break experience, make any desired adjustments, and prepare for subsequent hard breaks.

Feel free to use this worksheet to center yourself and clarify your goals, not only as you embark on your Sabbath experience, but as many times as you want or need to in the coming months and years.

Section One: Questions About Your Life as It Is Now

QUESTIONS TO ASK YOURSELF:

1. When was the last time my phone was off for 24 hours?
2. Did I respond to any work-related emails or texts last weekend? On my last vacation?
3. When was the last time I took a nap, or rested in the middle of the day?
4. When was the last time I read for pleasure?
5. When was the last day when I had no activities scheduled?
6. If I had one day off, what would I want to do?
7. What worries me about taking a Sabbath?

QUESTIONS TO ASK YOUR PARTNER/FRIEND/SPOUSE/CHILD:

1. Am I present when I'm with you, or am I distracted by work/technology?
2. How often do I talk about work?
3. Do you get stressed over managing your digital life?
4. What non-technology-aided activity do you wish we did more of?
5. What worries you about taking a Sabbath?
6. What regular activities would you like to do every Sabbath?
7. What would make a Sabbath special to you?

Things you want to work on and concrete steps to take *(e.g., turn off phone on Saturday morning, don't bring phone to dinner table, build in non-work, non-technology time on weekends)*.

1. _____

2. _____

3. _____

4. _____

5. _____

6. _____

7. _____

Section Two: Preparing for Sabbath

Ground rules for your hard break: the first four weeks. *(Remember, start with baby steps. Set reasonable expectations. Don't be so ambitious that adhering to your Sabbath ground rules becomes as stressful as your workweek. If you are taking a Sabbath with other people, work on this list in collaboration with them.)*

1. _____

2. _____

3. _____

4. _____

5. _____

6. _____

7. _____

What to do in case of emergencies:

1. What would I have to do to shut my phone off for a day?
2. Who do I want to warn that my phone will be off?
3. How will people reach me in case of emergency?
4. If I don't shut off my phone, can I turn off all notifications?

5. What technology solutions exist so my phone can remain on, but I'm not checking it constantly or taking in work-related communications?
6. In which situations would I violate my hard break?
7. How can I stay in touch with loved ones during a Sabbath?

Section Three: Reflecting on Your Sabbath Experience

How did your ground rules go? *(For each ground rule you listed above, write a sentence or two saying whether you adhered to it; and, whether you adhered to it or not, what your experience of it was.)*

1. _____

2. _____

3. _____

4. _____

5. _____

6. _____

7. _____

What experiences, thoughts, or feelings did you notice during your hard break that were different from what happens on a typical day in your life?

Ground rules for your hard break: the next four weeks. *(Now that you've had four weeks of Sabbath, how do you want to modify your ground rules? Add more? Take some away? Swap some out?)*

1. _____

2. _____

3. _____

4. _____

5. _____

6. _____

7. _____

Acknowledgments

There are many people to thank for this book. Here are a few.

Mike Silverander, thank you for helping me take a very raw draft of the book and put some real structure to it. Your time and counsel were very much appreciated.

Matthew Sharpe, your deft touch, keen eye, and kind encouragement took this book to another level.

Thank you to all the people interviewed for this book, including Brad Feld, Matt Auron, Senator Joseph Lieberman, Dan Shapiro, Gary Sabin, Barrie Lindahl, Dr. Marcus Elliott, David Sullivan, and Tony Crabbe.

Thank you to my advance readers, who gave valuable feedback and edits: David Cygielman, Rabbi Peter Berg, Guy Spier, Caroline Farrell, David Sullivan, and my wife, Valerie Edelheit. I want to especially thank Jeremy Bodenhamer, whose insights and detailed comments were simply invaluable.

Myka Cygielman, thank you for coming up with the title of the book.

Thanks to Rohit Bhargava and Marnie McMahon at IdeaPress for everything you did to make this book a reality. It has been a pleasure working under your publishing house.

A big thank you to my mother, Peggy Edelheit, and my brother, Marc Edelheit, for inspiring me to write my own book. You showed me the way.

Finally, I want to thank everyone who, over the past three years, encouraged and humored me while I wrestled with and wrote this book.

ENDNOTES

1 "overwork," *Oxford English Dictionary.* http://www.oed.com/view/ Entry/135388?rskey=hnJ6SR&result=2&isAdvanced=false#eid (accessed January 10, 2018).

2 John Pencavel, "The Productivity of Working Hours." *The Institute for the Study of Labor,* April 2014. http://ftp.iza.org/dp8129.pdf

3 Marguerite Ward, "A Brief History of the 8-hour Workday, Which Changed How Americans Work." *CNBC,* May 3, 2017. https://www. cnbc.com/2017/05/03/how-the-8-hour-workday-changed-how-americans-work.html

4 "Hours Worked." OECD.com. https://data.oecd.org/emp/hours-worked.htm (accessed January 10, 2018).

5 Ben Steverman, "Americans Work 25% More than Europeans, Study Finds." *Bloomberg News,* October 18, 2016. https://www.bloomberg. com/news/articles/2016-10-18/americans-work-25-more-than-europeans-study-finds

6 "Report of the Presidential Commission on the Space Shuttle Challenger Accident. Volume 2: Appendix G – Human Factor Analysis." *National Aeronautics and Space Administration.* http://history.nasa.gov/ rogersrep/v2appg.htm (accessed January 10, 2018).

[7] Pencavel, "The Productivity of Working Hours."

[8] Marshall Allen and Olga Pierce, "Medical Errors Are No. 3 Cause of U.S. Deaths, Researchers Say." *NPR*, May 3, 2016. http://www.npr.org/sections/health-shots/2016/05/03/476636183/death-certificates-undercount-toll-of-medical-errors

[9] Pencavel, "The Productivity of Working Hours."

[10] Waldemar Karwowski, ed., *International Encyclopedia of Ergonomics and Human Factors, Second Edition* (New York: CRC Press, 2006), 717.

[11] "New Hours-of-Service Safety Regulations to Reduce Truck Driver Fatigue Begin Today." *Federal Motor Carrier Safety Administration*, July 1, 2013. https://www.fmcsa.dot.gov/newsroom/new-hours-service-safety-regulations-reduce-truck-driver-fatigue-begin-today

[12] Ron Friedman, "Working Too Hard Makes Leading More Difficult." *Harvard Business Review*, December 30, 2014. https://hbr.org/2014/12/working-too-hard-makes-leading-more-difficult

[13] Claire C. Caruso et al., "Overtime and Extended Work Shifts: Recent Findings on Illnesses, Injuries, and Health Behaviors," *Centers for Disease Control and Prevention*, April 2004. https://www.cdc.gov/niosh/docs/2004-143/pdfs/2004-143.pdf

[14] Thu-Huong Ha, "This Is What 365 Days without a Vacation Does to your Health." *Quartz Media*, September 5, 2015. https://qz.com/485226/this-is-what-365-days-without-a-vacation-does-to-your-health/

[15] Sarah Green Carmichael, "Working Long Hours Makes Us Drink More." *Harvard Business Review*, April 10, 2015. https://hbr.org/2015/04/working-long-hours-makes-us-drink-more

[16] "The State of American Vacation 2017." *Project Time Off*. https://www.projecttimeoff.com/state-american-vacation-2017 (accessed January 10, 2018).

[17] "Glassdoor Survey Finds Americans Forfeit Half of Their Paid Vacation/Time Off." *Glassdoor*, May 24, 2017. https://www.glassdoor.com/press/glassdoor-survey-finds-americans-forfeit-earned-vacation-paid-time/

18 Aimee Picchi, "Why Americans Take Only Half Their Vacation Time." *CBS News*, April 4, 2014. http://www.cbsnews.com/news/why-americans-take-only-half-their-vacation-time/

19 Paul Wolfe, "Why Americans Don't Take Time Off: A Data-Driven Answer." *Indeed Blog*, September 22, 2016. http://blog.indeed.com/2016/09/22/how-to-encourage-employee-time-off/

20 Anders Melin and Ben Steverman, "A Way for Workers to Trade in Unused Vacation." *WorkforceXpert*. http://www.workforcexpert.com/a-way-for-workers-to-trade-in-unused-vacation (accessed January 10, 2018).

21 Robert C. Pozen, "Stop Working All Those Long Hours." *Lifehacker*, June 20, 2012. http://lifehacker.com/5919586/stop-working-all-those-long-hours

22 Erin Reid, "Why Some Men Pretend to Work 80-hour Weeks." *Harvard Business Review*, April 28, 2015. https://hbr.org/2015/04/why-some-men-pretend-to-work-80-hour-weeks

23 Picchi, "Why Americans Take Only Half Their Vacation Time."

24 Chris Taylor, "Three Ways to Avoid Guilt Over Taking a Vacation." *Reuters*, September 1, 2015. http://www.reuters.com/article/us-employment-vacations-guilt-idUSKCN0R143C20150901

25 "Why High Earners Work Longer Hours." *The National Bureau of Economic Research*. http://www.nber.org/digest/jul06/w11895.html (accessed January 10, 2018).

26 Doug Page, "NYT and WSJ: the Industry's Last Newspaper War?" *News & Tech*, February 26, 2013. http://newsandtech.com/columnists/article_4cbfda2c-8051-11e2-adb0-001a4bcf887a.html

27 Hilary Potkewitz, "Why 4 a.m. Is The Most Productive Hour." *The Wall Street Journal*, August 23, 2016. http://www.wsj.com/articles/why-4-a-m-is-the-most-productive-hour-1471971861

28 Jena McGregor, "How 'Busyness' Became a Bona Fide Status Symbol." *The Washington Post*, December 20, 2016. https://www.washingtonpost.com/news/on-leadership/wp/2016/12/20/how-busyness-became-a-bona-fide-status-symbol/?utm_term=.c93bfb7eb9e8

[29] Joan C. Williams, "Why Men Work So Many Hours." *Harvard Business Review,* May 29, 2013. https://hbr.org/2013/05/why-men-work-so-many-hours

[30] Derek Thompson, "The Free-time Paradox in America." *The Atlantic,* September 13, 2016. https://www.theatlantic.com/business/archive/2016/09/the-free-time-paradox-in-america/499826/

[31] "The Zeigarnik Effect." *Psyblog,* February 8, 2011. http://www.spring.org.uk/2011/02/the-zeigarnik-effect.php

[32] "Tips for Leaving Work Behind This Vacation." *The Wall Street Journal,* July 15, 2016. http://blogs.wsj.com/briefly/2016/07/15/tips-for-leaving-work-behind-this-vacation-at-a-glance/

[33] Rachel Feintzeig, "Feeling Burned Out at Work? Join the Club." *The Wall Street Journal,* February 28, 2017. https://www.wsj.com/articles/feeling-burned-out-at-work-join-the-club-1488286801

[34] Ha, "This Is What 365 Days without a Vacation Does to your Health."

[35] Carmichael, "Working Long Hours Makes Us Drink More."

[36] Catherine Saint Louis, "Researchers Link Longer Work Hours and Stroke Risk." *The New York Times,* August 19, 2015. http://well.blogs.nytimes.com/2015/08/19/researchers-link-longer-work-hours-and-stroke-risk/

[37] Valentina Zarya, "Working Long Hours Is Way Worse for Women's Health than for Men's." *Fortune,* June 17, 2016. http://fortune.com/2016/06/17/women-health-work/

[38] Carmichael, "Working Long Hours Makes Us Drink More."

[39] Caruso et al., "Overtime and Extended Work Shifts."

[40] Edmond S. Higgins, "Is Mental Health Declining in the U.S.?" *Scientific American,* January 1, 2017. https://www.scientificamerican.com/article/is-mental-health-declining-in-the-u-s/

41 "Workforce Mental Health Plays a Major Role in a Company's Productivity, Safety and Bottom Line." *Charlotte Business Journal*, September 15, 2016. https://www.bizjournals.com/charlotte/news/2016/09/15/workforce-mental-health-plays-a-major-role-in-a.html

42 Charlotte Lieberman, "What You're Hiding from When You Constantly Check Your Phone." *Harvard Business Review*, January 19, 2016. https://hbr.org/2016/01/what-youre-hiding-from-when-you-constantly-check-your-phone

43 "Road Trip! Health Net Points Out the Benefit of Vacations." *Health Net*. https://www.healthnet.com/portal/home/content/iwc/home/articles/health_benefits_of_vacations.action (accessed January 11, 2018).

44 Dustin Moskovitz, "Work Hard, Live Well." *Medium*, August 19, 2015. https://medium.com/life-learning/work-hard-live-well-ead-679cb506d

45 Tomasz Tunguz, "What I Learned from Complete Burnout at Work." *Tomasz Tunguz*, January 11, 2017. http://tomtunguz.com/lessons-from-my-first-burnout/

46 Moskovitz, "Work Hard, Live Well."

47 Taylor Lorenz, "How Asana Built the Best Company Culture in Tech." *Fast Company*, March 29, 2017. https://www.fastcompany.com/3069240/how-asana-built-the-best-company-culture-in-tech

48 Moskovitz, "Work Hard, Live Well."

49 Scott Weiss, "Success at Work, Failure at Home." *Medium*, September 24, 2015. https://medium.com/working-parents-in-america/success-at-work-failure-at-home-f1d6f5d8d92f

50 Eric Barker, "This Is How to Stop Checking Your Phone: 5 Secrets from Research." *Barking Up the Wrong Tree*. https://www.bakadesuyo.com/2017/03/how-to-stop-checking-your-phone/ (accessed January 11, 2018).

51 Michael Winnick, "Putting a Finger on Our Phone Obsession." *dscout*, June 16, 2016. https://blog.dscout.com/mobile-touches

[52] Alex Fradera, "The Psychological Toll of Being Off-Duty but 'On Call.'" The British Psychological Society *Research Digest*, September 10, 2015. http://digest.bps.org.uk/2015/09/the-psychological-toll-of-being-off.html

[53] S. Sonnetag et. al., "Staying Well and Engaged When Demands AreHigh: the Role of Psychological Detachment." *PubMed*, September 2010. https://www.ncbi.nlm.nih.gov/pubmed/20718528

[54] Tony Crabbe. *Busy: How to Thrive in a World of Too Much* (New York: Grand Central Publishing, 2015), 133.

[55] Deena Shanker, "Social Media Are Driving Americans Insane." *Bloomberg*, February 23, 2017. https://www.bloomberg.com/news/articles/2017-02-23/social-media-is-driving-americans-insane

[56] Matthew Diebel and Maya Vidon, "Here's Another Reason to Move to France: No After-work Emails." *USA Today*, January 4, 2017. https://www.usatoday.com/story/news/world/2017/01/04/heres-another-reason-move-france-no-after-work-emails/96148338/

[57] Eileen Carey, "How One Founder Went Dark on Social Media and Found the Light." *Mattermark*, December 13, 2016. https://mattermark.com/one-founder-went-dark-social-media-found-light/

[58] Robinson Meyer, "How Instagram Opened a Ruthless New Chapter in the Teen Photo Wars." *The Atlantic*, September 1, 2016. https://www.theatlantic.com/technology/archive/2016/09/how-one-teen-uses-instagram-and-snapchat-stories/498254/

[59] Gail Rosenblum, "How Some St. Paul College Students Are Learning to Connect without Cellphones." *Star Tribune*, October 21, 2016. http://www.startribune.com/minnesota-students-are-learning-to-connect-without-cellphones/397828311/

[60] Devorah Heitner, "Kids Don't Always Love Technology." *EdSurge*, September 7, 2016. https://www.edsurge.com/news/2016-09-07-kids-don-t-always-love-technology

[61] "More U.S. Middle School Students Dying of Suicide than Car Crashes, CDC Finds." *CBC News*, November 4, 2016. http://www.cbc.ca/news/health/suicide-stats-1.3836292

[62] Diana Kapp, "Why Are Palo Alto's Kids Killing Themselves?" *San Francisco Magazine,* May 22, 2016. http://www.modernluxury.com/san-francisco/story/why-are-palo-altos-kids-killing-themselves

[63] Andrea Petersen, "Students Flood College Mental Health Centers." *The Wall Street Journal,* October 10, 2016. http://www.wsj.com/articles/students-flood-college-mental-health-centers-1476120902

[64] Jean Twenge, "Teenage Depression and Suicide Are Way Up—and So Is Smartphone Use." *The Washington Post,* November 19, 2017. https://www.washingtonpost.com/national/health-science/teenage-depression-and-suicide-are-way-up--and-so-is-smartphone-use/2017/11/17/624641ea-ca13-11e7-8321-481fd63f174d_story.html?utm_term=.8c066d6fcd3c

[65] Jessica Stillman, "Facebook's Founding President: Facebook is Hurting Our Brains." *Inc.,* November 10, 2017. https://www.inc.com/jessica-stillman/facebooks-founding-president-on-stage-yesterday-we-created-a-monster.html

[66] Minda Zetlin, "Former Facebook VP Says Social Media Is Ripping Us Apart and We Should All Take a Hard Break." *Inc.,* December 12, 2017. https://www.inc.com/minda-zetlin/former-facebook-vp-says-social-media-is-ripping-us-apart-we-should-all-take-a-hard-break.html

[67] Christopher Mele, "Levi Felix, a Proponent of Disconnecting from Technology, Dies at 32." *The New York Times,* January 12, 2017. https://www.nytimes.com/2017/01/12/us/obituary-levi-felix-digital-detox.html?_r=3

[68] Marina Lopes, "We're So Addicted to Our Gadgets that 'Unplugged' Tourism Is Booming. *Motherboard,* October 7, 2016. http://motherboard.vice.com/read/tourism-is-capitalizing-on-our-addiction-to-technology-with-unplugged-hotels

[69] Seth Godin, "When Your Phone Uses You." *Seth's Blog,* December 30, 2016. http://sethgodin.typepad.com/seths_blog/2016/12/when-your-phone-uses-you.html

[70] "Screen Free – Technology Policy." *Beber Camp.* http://www.beber-camp.com/current-families/getting-ready-for-camp/screen-free-technology-policy/ (accessed January 11, 2018).

71 Jordan Cooper, "On Burning Out." *Jordan Cooper's Blog*, November 5, 2016. https://jordancooper.blog/2016/11/05/on-burning-out/

72 Sam Harnett, "For the Productivity-Obsessed of Silicon Valley, Coffee Alone May Not Cut It Anymore. *Marketplace*, January 16, 2017. http://www.marketplace.org/2017/01/16/business/nootropics-market-taps-desire-be-more-productive

73 Ha, "This Is What 365 Days without a Vacation Does to your Health."

74 Biz Carson, "There's a Dark Side to Startups, and It Haunts 30% of the World's Most Brilliant People." *Business Insider*, July 1, 2015. http://www.businessinsider.com/austen-heinzs-suicide-and-depression-in-startups-2015-7

75 Justin Karter, "Percentage of Americans on Antidepressants Nearly Doubles." *Mad in America*, November 6, 2015. https://www.madinamerica.com/2015/11/percentage-of-americans-on-antidepressants-nearly-doubles/

76 Andrew Ross Sorkin, "Reflections on Stress and Long Hours on Wall Street." *The New York Times*, June 1, 2015. https://www.nytimes.com/2015/06/02/business/dealbook/reflections-on-stress-and-long-hours-on-wall-street.html?_r=0

77 Emily Glazer and Daniel Huang, "J.P. Morgan to Workaholics: Knock It Off." *The Wall Street Journal*, January 21, 2016. https://www.wsj.com/articles/j-p-morgan-chase-tells-investment-bankers-to-take-weekends-off-1453384738

78 Sabrina Tavernise, "U.S. Suicide Rate Surges to a New 30-Year High." *The New York Times*, April 22, 2016. https://www.nytimes.com/2016/04/22/health/us-suicide-rate-surges-to-a-30-year-high.html

79 Joseph I. Lieberman, *The Gift of Rest: Rediscovering the Beauty of the Sabbath* (New York: Howard Books, 2012), 28.

80 Jonathan Raymond, *Good Authority: How to Become the Leader Your Team Is Waiting For* (Washington, D.C.: IdeaPress Publishing, 2016), 187.

81 Mark Beech, "The Power of Sleep: J.J. Watt Knows How to Turn It On and Turn It Off." *Sports Illustrated*, April 25, 2016. https://www.si.com/nfl/2016/04/25/jj-watt-houston-texans-workout-gatorade

82 Cheri D. Mah et. al., "The Effects of Sleep Extension on the Athletic Performance of Collegiate Basketball Players." *PubMed Central*, July 1, 2011. https://www.ncbi.nlm.nih.gov/pmc/articles/PMC3119836/

83 "Aroldis Chapman Criticizes How Joe Maddon Used Him Late in World Series." *CBS Chicago*, December 16, 2016. http://chicago.cbslocal.com/2016/12/16/aroldis-chapman-cubs-joe-maddon/

84 Wayne Wood, "Vanderbilt Study Indicates Fatigue and Loss of Sleep Take Predictable Toll on Baseball Players Over Course of Season. *Vanderbilt*, June 4, 2013. https://news.vanderbilt.edu/2013/06/04/vanderbilt-study-indicates-fatigue-and-loss-of-sleep-takes-predictable-toll-on-baseball-players-over-season/

85 Katie Brown, "Resting, the Strategic Way." *Climbing*, June 15, 2012. http://www.climbing.com/skills/resting-the-strategic-way/

86 Paul Kimmage, "Paul Kimmage Meets Rory McIlroy: The Truth About the Olympics, Close Friendship with Tiger and the Important Things in Life." *The Independent*, June 8, 2017. http://www.independent.ie/sport/golf/paul-kimmage-meets-rory-mcilroy-the-truth-about-the-olympics-close-friendship-with-tiger-and-the-important-things-in-life-35349397.html

87 "LeBron James in Social Media Shutdown Mode During NBA Playoffs." *USA Today*, April 21, 2015. https://www.usatoday.com/story/sports/nba/2015/04/21/lebron-james-in-social-media-shutdown-mode-during-playoffs/26125571/

88 Lisa Evans, "Why Taking a Vacation Can Make You Better at Your Job." *Fast Company*, May 22, 2014. http://www.fastcompany.com/3030865/work-smart/why-taking-a-vacation-can-make-you-better-at-your-job

89 Leigh Gallagher, "Burned Out at Work? Learn How to Vacation Like J.P. Morgan." *Fortune*, August 18, 2017. http://fortune.com/2017/08/18/j-p-morgan-vacation/

90 Brian Scudamore, "We Ban Employees from Email During Vacations. Here's Why." *Inc.*, December 12, 2016. http://www.inc.com/
brian-scudamore/we-ban-employees-from-email-during-vacations-
heres-why.html

91 Brian Scudamore, "Tips for Leaving Work Behind This Vacation."
The Wall Street Journal, July 15, 2016. http://blogs.wsj.com/brief-
ly/2016/07/15/tips-for-leaving-work-behind-this-vacation-at-a-
glance/

92 Madeline Diamond, "This Company Pays Its Employees $7500
to Vacation Tech Free." *The Huffington Post*, June 24, 2016. http://
www.huffingtonpost.com/entry/company-pays-employees-to-vaca-
tion-tech-free_us_576d5348e4b0f16832395581

93 "The Best Places to Work: 2016." *Outside*, November 15, 2016. http://
www.outsideonline.com/2134736/best-places-work-2016

94 Ha, "This Is What 365 Days without a Vacation Does to your Health."

95 "The High Price of Silence: Analyzing the Business Implications of an
Under-Vacationed Workforce." *Project Time Off.* https://www.project-
timeoff.com/research/high-price-silence (accessed February 6, 2018).

96 Ferris Jabr, "Why Your Brain Needs More Downtime." *Scientific American*, October 15, 2013. https://www.scientificamerican.com/article/
mental-downtime/

97 Brian Scudamore, "Why Successful People Spend 10 Hours a Week
Just Thinking." *Medium*, April 26, 2016. https://medium.com/
the-mission/why-successful-people-spend-10-hours-a-week-just-
thinking-79a5b16eb404

98 David Wolpe, "Lasting Power." *The New York Jewish Week*, March 8,
2017. http://blogs.timesofisrael.com/lasting-power/

99 Jim Loehr and Tony Schwartz. *The Power of Full Engagement: Managing Energy, Not Time, Is the Key to High Performance and Personal
Renewal* (New York: Free Press, 2005), 37.

100 *ibid.*, 12.

101 *Goodreads.* https://www.goodreads.com/quotes/230531-opportunities-to-find-deeper-powers-within-ourselves-come-when-life (accessed January 14, 2018).

102 Rebecca Greenfield, "The $100,000 Anti-burnout Program for CEOs." *Bloomberg,* March 27, 2017. https://www.bloomberg.com/news/articles/2017-03-27/the-100-000-anti-burnout-program-for-ceos

103 Jason Lengstorf, "How to Know If You've Joined a Cult." *JL.* https://lengstorf.com/overkill-cult/ (accessed January 15, 2018).

104 Tim Kreider, "The 'Busy' Trap." *The New York Times,* June 12, 2012. https://opinionator.blogs.nytimes.com/2012/06/30/the-busy-trap/?_r=0

105 Crabbe, *Busy,* 25.

106 *ibid.,* 45

107 Jeff Iliff, "One More Reason to Get a Good Night's Sleep." *TED.* https://www.ted.com/talks/jeff_iliff_one_more_reason_to_get_a_good_night_s_sleep/transcript?language=en (accessed January 15, 2018).

108 Robert Epstein, "The Empty Brain." *Aeon,* May 18, 2016. https://aeon.co/essays/your-brain-does-not-process-information-and-it-is-not-a-computer

109 Jabr, "Why Your Brain Needs More Downtime."

110 Crabbe, *Busy,* 83.

111 Carmen Nobel, "Reflecting on Work Improves Job Performance." *Harvard Business School Working Knowledge,* May 5, 2014. http://hbswk.hbs.edu/item/reflecting-on-work-improves-job-performance

112 Peter Thiel, with Blake Masters, *Zero to One: Notes on Startups, or How to Build the Future* (New York: Crown Business, 2014), 42.

113 Loehr and Schwartz, *The Power of Full Engagement,* 96–97.

114 Jacquelyn Smith, "72% of People Get Their Best Ideas in the Shower—Here's Why." *Business Insider,* January 14, 2016. http://www.businessinsider.com/why-people-get-their-best-ideas-in-the-shower-2016-1

[115] Kia Kokalitcheva, "Lin-Manuel Miranda Thought 'Hamilton' Would Only Appeal to History Teachers." *Fortune*, September 23, 2016. http://fortune.com/2016/09/23/lin-manuel-miranda-hamilton-40-under-40/

[116] Sierra Marquina, "Kanye West Got Rid of His Cell Phone So He Has More 'Air to Create." *Us Weekly*, September 14, 2016. http://www.usmagazine.com/celebrity-news/news/kanye-west-gets-rid-of-cell-phone-to-create-

[117] Nash Jenkins, "Kanye West's 40-Minute Lecture at Oxford University Is Now Available Online." *Time*, December 9, 2015. http://time.com/4142065/kanye-west-oxford-guild-society-speech/

[118] Wayne Muller, *Sabbath: Finding Rest, Renewal, and Delight in Our Busy Lives* (New York: Bantam, 2000), 189.

[119] Zaria Gorvett, "What You Can Learn from Einstein's Quirky Habits." *BBC*, June 12, 2017. http://www.bbc.com/future/story/20170612-what-you-can-learn-from-einsteins-quirky-habits

[120] Morgan Housel, "Lazy Work, Good Work." *Collaborative Fund*, December 15, 2016. http://www.collaborativefund.com/blog/lazy-work-good-work/

[121] Robert A. Guth, "In Secret Hideaway, Bill Gates Ponders Microsoft's Future." *The Wall Street Journal*, March 20, 2005. http://www.wsj.com/articles/SB111196625830690477

[122] Crabbe, *Busy*, 220.

[123] Frank Bruni, "The Myth of Quality Time." *The New York Times*, September 5, 2015. https://www.nytimes.com/2015/09/06/opinion/sunday/frank-bruni-the-myth-of-quality-time.html

[124] Claire Cain Miller, "Stressed, Tired, Rushed: A Portrait of the Modern Family." *The New York Times*, November 4, 2015. https://www.nytimes.com/2015/11/05/upshot/stressed-tired-rushed-a-portrait-of-the-modern-family.html

[125] Lisa Damour, "What Do Teenagers Want? Potted Plant Parents. *The New York Times*, December 14, 2016. http://mobile.nytimes.com/2016/12/14/well/family/what-do-teenagers-want-potted-plant-parents.html

126 Michael D. Resnick et. al., "Protecting Adolescents From Harm: Findings From the National Longitudinal Study on Adolescent Health." *ResearchGate*, September 1997. https://www.researchgate. net/publication/13927256_Protecting_Adolescents_From_Harm-Findings_From_the_National_Longitudinal_Study_on_Adoles-cent_Health

127 Claudia Wallis, "The New Science of Happiness." *Time*, January 9, 2005. http://content.time.com/time/magazine/arti-cle/0,9171,1015832,00.html

128 Crabbe, *Busy*, 181.

129 Robert Waldinger, "What Makes a Good Life? Lessons from the Longest Study on Happiness. *TED*. https://www.ted.com/talks/rob-ert_waldinger_what_makes_a_good_life_lessons_from_the_lon-gest_study_on_happiness/transcript (accessed on January 16, 2018).

130 Crabbe, *Busy*, 181.

131 Nir Eyal, "Happiness Hack: This One Ritual Made Me Much Happi-er." *LinkedIn*, February 18, 2016. https://www.linkedin.com/pulse/happiness-hack-one-ritual-made-me-much-happier-nir-eyal

132 Dhruv Khullar, "How Social Isolation Is Killing Us." *The New York Times*, December 22, 2016. https://www.nytimes.com/2016/12/22/upshot/how-social-isolation-is-killing-us.html?_r=0

133 John F. Helliwell and Haifang Huang, "Comparing the Happiness Effects of Real and On-line Friends." *Public Library of Science*, September 3, 2013. http://journals.plos.org/plosone/article?id=10.1371/journal.pone.0072754

134 "The David Rubinstein Show: Warren Buffett." *Bloomberg*, November 4, 2016. https://www.bloomberg.com/news/videos/2016-11-04/the-david-rubenstein-show-warren-buffett

135 Hal E. Hershfield and Cassie Mogilner Holmes, "What Should You Choose, Time or Money?" *The New York Times*, September 9, 2016. http://www.nytimes.com/2016/09/11/opinion/sunday/what-should-you-choose-time-or-money.html?_r=1

136 Loehr and Schwartz, *The Power of Full Engagement*, 137.

137 Manning Feinlieb, M.D. et. al., *Vital Statistics of the United States 1979, Volume III: Marriage and Divorce* (Hyattsville, MD: National Center for Health Statistics, 1984), 2–5. https://www.cdc.gov/nchs/data/vsus/mgdv79_3.pdf

138 A. J. Norton and L. F. Miller, "Marriage, Divorce, and Remarriage in the 1990s." *PubMed*, October 1992. https://www.ncbi.nlm.nih.gov/pubmed/12345021

139 Matthew Sleeth, *24/6: A Prescription for a Healthier, Happier Life* (Carol Stream, IL: Tyndale House Publishers, 2012), 8–9.

140 Brett and Kate McKay, "The Power of Ritual: the Rocket Booster of Personal Change, Transformation, and Progress." *The Art of Manliness*, January 28, 2014. http://www.artofmanliness.com/2014/01/28/the-power-of-ritual-the-booster-rocket-of-personal-change-transformation-and-progress/

141 Francesca Gino and Michael I. Norton, "Why Rituals Work." *Scientific American*, May 14, 2013. https://www.scientificamerican.com/article/why-rituals-work/

142 Heidi Grant, "New Research: Rituals Make Us Value Things More." *Harvard Business Review*, December 12, 2013. https://hbr.org/2013/12/new-research-rituals-make-us-value-things-more-https://dash.harvard.edu/bitstream/handle/1/10686852/vohs,%20wang,%20gino,%20norton_rituals-enhance-consumption.pdf?sequence=1

143 Maryann Jacobsen, "5 Ways to Cultivate an Appreciation of Food in Your Child." *Maryann Jacobsen*, October 21, 2015. http://www.maryannjacobsen.com/2015/10/5-ways-to-cultivate-an-appreciation-of-food-in-your-child/

144 Daniel Mochon et. al., "Getting Off the Hedonic Treadmill, One Step at a Time: the Effect of Regular Religious Practice and Exercise on Well-being." *Journal of Economic Psychology*, October 30, 2007. http://www.people.hbs.edu/mnorton/mochon%20norton%20ariely%202008.pdf

145 Charles Duhigg, *The Power of Habit: Why We Do What We Do in Life and Business* (New York: Random House, 2014), 100–101.

[146] *ibid.*, 20.

[147] *ibid.*, 215–222.

[148] "keystone." Dictionary.com. http://www.dictionary.com/browse/keystone (accessed January 18, 2018).

[149] Duhigg, *The Power of Habit*, 100–101.

[150] *ibid.*, 112.

[151] Duhigg, "How 'Keystone Habits' Transformed a Corporation." *The Huffington Post*, February 27, 2012. https://www.huffingtonpost.com/charles-duhigg/the-power-of-habit_b_1304550.html

[152] "Chick-fil-A Reaches Milestone with 2000th Restaurant Opening." *The Chicken Wire*, February 16, 2016. https://thechickenwire.chickfil-a.com/News/ChickfilA-Reaches-Milestone-with-2000th-Restaurant-Opening

[153] Vickey Mabrey and Mary Marsh, "How to Win Customers...by Closing." *ABC News*, September 23, 2009. http://abcnews.go.com/Nightline/10Commandments/ten-commandments-sabbath-holy-chick-fil-a-closes-sundays/story?id=8570384

[154] Hayley Peterson, "Why Chick-fil-A Is Beating Every Other Fast Food Chain in the U.S." *Business Insider*, October 4, 2016. http://www.businessinsider.com/why-chick-fil-a-is-so-successful-2016-10

[155] Madeline Farber, "This Southern Icon is America's Favorite Fast Food Restaurant." *Fortune*, June 21, 2016. http://fortune.com/2016/06/21/chick-fil-a-favorite-fast-food-restaurant/

[156] Phil W. Hudson, "Chick-fil-A to Double Employee Scholarship Investment." *Atlanta Business Journal*, September 21, 2016. http://www.bizjournals.com/atlanta/news/2016/09/21/chick-fil-a-to-double-employee-scholarship.html

[157] Kevin Kruse, "How Chick-fil-A Created a Culture that Lasts." *Forbes*, December 8, 2015. https://www.forbes.com/sites/kevinkruse/2015/12/08/how-chick-fil-a-created-a-culture-that-lasts/#15810313602e

158 "Chick-fil-A." *Glassdoor*. https://www.glassdoor.com/Overview/ Working-at-Chick-fil-A-EI_IE5873.11,22.htm (accessed January 18, 2018).

159 "Kentucky Fried Chicken." *Glassdoor*. https://www.glassdoor.com/ Reviews/kentucky-fried-chicken-reviews-SRCH_KE0,22.htm (accessed February 7, 2018).

160 "Chick-fil-A to Source 100 Percent Cage-free Eggs." March 9, 2016. https://thechickenwire.chick-fil-a.com/News/Chick-fil-A-to-Source-100-Percent-Cage-Free-Eggs

161 Emma Green, "Chick-fil-A: Selling Chicken with a Side of God." *The Atlantic*, September 8, 2014. https://www.theatlantic.com/business/archive/2014/09/chick-fil-a-selling-chicken-with-a-side-of-god/379776/

162 Lieberman, *The Gift of Rest*, 208.

163 *ibid.*, ix.

164 *ibid.*, 144.

165 *ibid.*, 34.

166 *ibid.*, 54.

167 *ibid.*, 52.

168 *ibid.*, 4.

169 *ibid.*, 50.

170 DeVon Franklin, *Produced by Faith: Enjoy Real Success Without Losing Your True Self* (New York: Howard Books, 2012), 106.

171 *ibid.*, 110.

172 *ibid.*, 194–195.

173 *ibid.*, 165.

174 *ibid.*, 106.

175 Joe Robinson, "Why Being a Workaholic Is Counterproductive." *Entrepreneur*, February 2013. https://www.entrepreneur.com/article/225444

[176] "The 100 Best Companies to Work for: Boston Consulting Group." *Fortune*, 2017. http://fortune.com/best-companies/the-boston-consulting-group-3/

[177] Marc Andreesen and Clayton Christensen, "Disruption in Business... and Life." *a16z podcast*, March 3, 2016. https://a16z.com/2016/03/03/disruption-clay-marc/

[178] "A Better Way to Work." *Boston Consulting Group*. http://www.bcg.com/careers/path/consulting/better-way-to-work.aspx (accessed January 18, 2018).

[179] Lieberman, *The Gift of Rest*, 28.

[180] *ibid.*, 169.

[181] *ibid.*, 2.

[182] Duhigg, *The Power of Habit*, 100–101.

[183] Spencer Rascoff, "Why Work-Life Balance Starts at the Top—and How to Achieve It." *Inc.*, August 17, 2018. https://www.inc.com/spencer-rascoff/3-ways-leaders-can-achieve-better-work-life-balanc.html

[184] McKay, "The Napping Habits of 8 Famous Men." *The Art of Manliness*, March 21, 2011. http://www.artofmanliness.com/2011/03/14/the-napping-habits-of-8-famous-men/

[185] McKay, "Unleash the Power of the Nap." *The Art of Manliness*, February 7, 2011. http://www.artofmanliness.com/2011/02/07/unleash-the-power-of-the-nap/

[186] Jonathan Safran Foer, *Eating Animals* (New York: Back Bay Books, 2010), 163.

[187] Cody C. Delistraty, "The Importance of Eating Together." *The Atlantic*, July 18, 2014. https://www.theatlantic.com/health/archive/2014/07/the-importance-of-eating-together/374256/

[188] Hannah Seligson, "How to Have a Dinner Party: Friends Not Required." *The New York Times*, December 14, 2016. https://mobile.nytimes.com/2016/12/14/fashion/dinner-party-apps.html

[189] Crabbe, *Busy*, 58.

190 Ruth Ann Atchley et. al., "Creativity in the Wild: Improving Creative Reasoning Through Immersion in Natural Settings." *Public Library of Science*, December 12, 2012. http://journals.plos.org/plosone/article?id=10.1371/journal.pone.0051474

191 Craig Dowden, "Steve Jobs Was Right About Walking." *Financial Post*, December 12, 2014. http://business.financialpost.com/executive/c-suite/steve-jobs-was-right-about-walking

192 K. Knop et. al., "Sport and Oxidative Stress in Oncology Patients." *PubMed*, December 2011. https://www.ncbi.nlm.nih.gov/pubmed/22095321

193 Abigail Wise, "Proof That Hiking Makes You Happier and Healthier." *The Huffington Post*, July 18, 2014. http://www.huffingtonpost.com/2014/07/18/how-taking-a-hike-can-mak_n_5584809.html

194 Lieberman, *The Gift of Rest*, 72

195 Frank Bruni, "The Myth of Quality Time." *The New York Times*, September 5, 2016. https://www.nytimes.com/2015/09/06/opinion/sunday/frank-bruni-the-myth-of-quality-time.html

196 Crabbe, *Busy*, 212.

197 "Inauguration of Zachary Taylor." *Wikipedia*. https://en.wikipedia.org/wiki/Inauguration_of_Zachary_Taylor (accessed January 18, 2018).

198 Andreesen and Christensen, "Disruption in Business... and Life."

199 Crabbe, *Busy*, 220.

200 McKay, "The Nature and Power of Ritual Series Conclusion: On Ritual Resistance." *The Art of Manliness*, January 28, 2014. http://www.artofmanliness.com/2014/01/28/the-nature-and-power-of-ritual-series-conclusion-on-ritual-resistance/

INDEX

Type 2 diabetes, link between long
work hours and, 42

U
Uncover Boss (TV show), 106
Undemanding, 105
Underperformance, of invesment
portfolio, 9
Unetaneh Tohkef, 197–198
United Auto Workers, 23

V
Vacations, 71
for Americans, 25–29
benefits of, 74
direct influence on health and safety,
43
guilt in taking, 28–29
legal reasons for offering, 25
need for, 25
paid, paid, 104–106
purpose of, 25
unused, 26–27, 31
Virganen, Marianna, 42
Virgil, 187

W
Waldinger, Robert, 130
Walk, taking in the park, 185–187
Watt, J. J., 95
Wealth, leisure and, 33
Weddings, 138
Weinberg, Steven, 123
Weiss, Scott, 46–47
Welch, J. C., 117
West, Kanye, 122–123, 193
Williams, Joan C., 35
Wolpe, David, 108
Women
overwork by, 35–36
work hours of, 42
Wooden, John, 178
Work, 14
counterproductive, 120
leak into non-work time, 36–37
Workaholics, 2

suicide in, 60–63
Workcations, 26, 31
Work emails
out-of-office, 64
time spent on, 27, 36, 49
Work engagement, job demands and,
50–51
Work force, changing demographics of
the, 126
Work habits, 14
Work hours, 14
asking for reduced, 28
link between long and type 2
diabetes, 42
of women, 42
Working
perils of not, 164–166
reasons for, 195–196, 203–204
Working long hours, as a heroic activity,
35–36
Working rich, 32–33
Work/life balance, 88, 90–91, 126,
165–166
Workplace, peer pressure in minimizing
time off, 27
Work quality, optics versus, 28
Work-related stress, 41
Work responsibilities, visualizing, 74
World War I, productivity in, 16, 17

X
X.com, 121

Y
Yom Kippurd, 8, 197

Z
Zeigarnik, Bluma, 39
Zeigarnik effect, 31, 38–40
"Zero Dark Thirty-23," 97
Zhitomirskiy, Ilya, 60
Zillow, 179
Zuckerberg, Mark, 60, 186
Zynga, 59–60